# CORVETTE GTP

TELECOR
CORVETTE
TELECOM
DELCO
Bravo
DELCO
BFGoodrich
T/A Radials
GEOSTAR
GEOSTAR
PEERLESS

# CORVETTE GTP

## Alex Gabbard

**Howell Press**

# CORVETTE GTP

by Alex Gabbard

Designed by Theresa Munt
Edited by Katherine A. Neale and Keri Moser

Library of Congress Cataloging-in-Publication Data

Gabbard, Alex.
    Corvette GTP/by Alex Gabbard.
    p. cm.
    Includes index.
    ISBN: 1-57427-057-5.

    1.Corvette automobile.    2.Automobile racing—United States—History.    I. Title.

TL215.C6G33 1996              629.222'2
                             QBI96-20075

Printed in Hong Kong
Published by Howell Press, Inc.,
1147 River Road, Suite 2,
Charlottesville, Virginia 22901.
Telephone: (804) 977-4006
First Printing

# CONTENTS

# GTP Origins: the Lola Racing Tradition

The marque of Lola is the work and inspiration of one man, Britain's Eric Broadley. In 1975, Lola Cars, Ltd. produced its one thousandth car; all were racing cars in one form or another. This figure assures that Broadley stands among the greatest sports-racing car designers of all time. Lola is among the premier marques on the short list of the world's most historic racing cars. Raced today in both leading-edge technology and vintage racing forms, Lola may be the all-time winningest marque among sports-racing cars of all classes.

The Lola racing tradition began with the little front engine 1.1-liter, 4-cylinder Mk I Lola-Climax of 1958 and evolved through the decades to become the racing cars featured in this book: the Lola T-600, T-710, and T-810. The concept of the rear engine Lola sports-racing car powered by an American V8 behind the driver began with the Lola GT of 1963. That was Broadley's first effort with such a car, and with great vision, he based his design on the Chevrolet small-block engine.

That first Lola GT came along at the time when Ford Motor Company launched its "Total Performance" era of racing. Once Ford settled on a plan to campaign prototype cars against the finest racing machines in the world, Eric Broadley and his Lola GT were tapped to be the beginning of Ford's effort. Soon, though, Broadley and Ford parted ways, and while Ford went on to win everything worth winning in the following years, including world champion-

ships, Broadley worked on what became the Lola T-70, introduced in 1966.

Once again, Broadley designed his latest sports-racing car for the Chevrolet V8 engine. The magnificently styled T-70, an open car (that led to the equally magnificent T-70 Mk IIIB coupe), was an instant success and was soon campaigned throughout the world of racing. Broadley's T-70 became firmly established among the finest purpose-built racing cars in the world. One of the drivers who successfully raced T-70s in the 1960s was Brian Redman, a driver who was to become a central figure in the history of the cars featured in this book. Redman's sterling credentials included wins on every major racetrack in the world, along with no fewer than sixteen championship titles driving Fords, Porsches, Ferraris, BMWs, and a variety of Chevrolet V8-powered racing cars.

By the late 1950s, the Chevrolet V8 engine was a fixture in American racing. The front engine Scarab, Echidna, Devin SS, and many other "specials" proved to be championship racing cars. Many European cars were improved with engine swaps that disposed of expensive and temperamental European engines in favor of the strong, reliable, and powerful Chevy. By the mid-1960s, the concept of placing the engine behind the driver proved highly successful with such cars as the Chaparral-2 machines campaigned by Texan Jim Hall. When the big-block Chevrolet V8 came on the scene, racing

**(opposite)** The magnificent Lola T-70 Mk IIIB of the late 1960s, the forebear of modern, highly sophisticated monocoque GTP cars.

**(below)** Mark Donohue led a Lola T-70 one-two victory in the 24-Hours of Daytona of 1969, defeating a swarm of factory Porsche prototypes.

A

B

cars turned up the heat with more than 200 horse-power more than the small-block. The McLaren M-series cars, with more than 740 HP, proved to be nearly invincible in the premier professional racing series of the time, the Canadian-American Challenge Cup series (the Can-Am), which drew the finest cars and drivers from all over the world to North American tracks.

Then the doldrums of the 1970s set in. With long gas lines and rapidly escalating gasoline prices, inter-est in racing declined and the big engines became dinosaurs. But racing continued, and the Chevrolet small-block V8, displacing 302 to 377 cubic inches, emerged more powerful than ever and roared back to the winner's circle.

While the Sports Car Club of America (SCCA) continued to promote racing primarily for amateurs in the late 1960s, the International Motor Sports Association (IMSA) was born in 1969 and initiated a fledgling series of races with an eye toward long-term growth into broad professional racing. IMSA grew rapidly and was soon the premier racing series in the United States.

In the early 1970s, the German cars from Porsche and BMW reigned supreme in IMSA GT racing. Then came the tube frame Chevy V8-powered Monza designed by Lee Dykstra and driven by Al Holbert to the IMSA championship. Holbert's name eventually became synonymous with Porsche and GTP victories. The IMSA Monza won six races in its debut season. The Dekon Monza racing car with its tubular frame, exotic suspension, and aggressive body only looked like the Chevrolet Monza. No longer were IMSA cars strictly based on production platforms. They could be purpose-built cars of virtu-ally any configuration. The flexibility of IMSA's rules was the catalyst that produced some of the most exciting racing ever seen anywhere. Top-shelf sports car racing was given a decidedly Chevrolet flair in 1976 and 1977 with Holbert and the Dekon Monzas. The following years were ruled by turbocharged Porsche 935s in every configuration conceivable. During this time Brian Redman raced and won in anything that could go fast, including three consecu-tive Formula 5000 championships on U.S. circuits

with Chevrolet V8-powered open wheel cars that rivaled world-class Formula One cars for absolute speed and lap times.

Based on IMSA's 1980 rules for Grand Touring (GT) class racing with production-based sports cars, Redman conceived the original Grand Touring Prototype (GTP) car. Being thoroughly familiar with Lola cars and Broadley's capability, and having raced current turbocharged Porsches, Redman recognized that a properly designed Lola prototype coupe pow-ered by a rear-mounted Chevrolet V8 engine would be superior to the prevailing Porsches. The concept produced a heated battle between normally aspirat-ed Chevrolet V8 engines and smaller-displacement turbocharged Porsche flat-six engines. More low-end torque gave the V8 quicker exits from turns and, consequently, lower lap times that proved superior to the best from Porsche.

When Redman introduced the first GTP car in the fifth race of the 1981 season at Laguna Seca on May 3, the brilliant yellow Cooke-Woods Racing Lola assured that IMSA GT racing would never be the same again. Redman won in the car's debut appear-ance against a field of seasoned professional drivers in well-developed cars that, suddenly, were obsolete. The very first Lola T-600, a total ground effect design package, proved Redman's judgment correct; he went on to win the IMSA GTP overall championship in the car's first season!

Gone with the roar of the American V8, Porsche's long tradition of dominating road racing was over. The era of the GTP began, and IMSA was the scene of the most rapid advances in motor racing history. Yet to come were new Porsches, BMWs, and Fords, and all sorts of chassis/engine combinations, in exciting racing that promised more with each pass-ing year. IMSA GT was racing at its very best.

Redman and the Cooke-Woods Lola T-600 caught the eye of everyone who wanted to race and win, and especially at the Chevrolet Division of General Motors. Factory engineers there were involved in reviving Chevrolet's interest in racing as a develop-ment exercise for future products, namely smaller engines and advanced computer-based electronic control systems. They used the aerodynamic enve-

**A.** Cap Chenoweth of Stowe, Vermont, keeps the faith with his Mk I Lola.

**B.** Refinements of the rear engine concept with deep Chevrolet engineering involvement came to fruition with Jim Hall's Chaparral-2. Here, Hap Sharp remembers their Sebring win in 1965.

lope of the current Corvette, but instead of racing with normally aspirated V8s, the Chevy men conceived a plan to race suitably developed production-based V6 engines. The Corvette nameplate was among America's most admired, and the Lola platform was ideally suited for the task, but power had to be increased substantially to make the Corvette GTP competitive.

Engine wizard Ryan Falconer was brought on to the project to fully develop the V6 in turbocharged form. With the help of two of the greatest minds in the business, Broadley and Falconer, the results were astounding. When the cars were placed in the hands of Rick Hendrick, one of NASCAR's premier racing team owners, all the ingredients for success were in place. The GM Goodwrench-sponsored Corvette GTP based on the Lola T-710 proved to be among the most powerful racing cars of all time. In the hands of brilliant drivers, among them Sarel Van Der Merwe of South Africa and America's Doc Bundy, the cars displayed all the ingredients of champions.

However, the pace of technological development in GTP racing was very rapid, and just as the Lola T-600 was soon surpassed, the Corvette GTP was also. Along the way, though, the Corvette GTP cars displayed much more capability than their number of wins attests. Since the cars were official GM/Chevrolet factory-backed entries, the engineers' primary interest in them was often at odds with winning races; testing for product development often took priority over winning races. Winning was always the goal of the Corvette GTP team, but not always the main goal of the factory.

A

B

*(opposite)* Bruce McLaren won the Can-Am in his M8B in 1969, and Denny Hulme won the Can-Am the following year in the M8D as shown here. Peter Revson won in the similar M8F in '71.

A. Al Unser competed with three-time Formula 5000 champion Brian Redman in this Chevrolet-powered Lola.

B. The Löwenbräu Special Porsches were a formidable team in 1985; superb cars, excellent preparation. Al Holbert won the IMSA Championship that year while co-driver Derek Bell won the World Endurance Championship, both taken by 962s.

# Chevrolet-powered Sports-racing Cars

The first application of Chevrolet's new 1955 V8 engine in road racing was an engine swap replacing a British four-banger. The car was an Alta-powered HWM (Hersham and Walton Motors) purchased by avid racer Bill Pollack when the car was sold by a Hollywood film studio. Famed engine equipment manufacturer Vic Edelbrock and friends made several modifications to the car to produce the HWM-Chevy. Pollack introduced this very powerful car at a road race held at Pebble Beach, California, in 1956. The car opened the gate to a vast array of Chevrolet small-block V8-powered sports-racing cars that followed. IMSA GT Prototype cars ran descendants of this engine thirty years later.

One of the first cars designed specifically for the Chevy small-block was Lance Reventlow's Scarab. The son of Woolworth heiress Barbara Hutton, Reventlow set up his own factory in Los Angeles to build competition cars. He had just turned twenty-one, and the cars he planned to build were intended to conquer the world. What they actually did was dominate American road racing and earn successive national championships.

The cars were financed by Reventlow and built by a team of expert racers like none seen before in this country. Ken Miles, well known builder, driver, and editor of a series of articles on how to build competitive sports cars, was commissioned to do the basic layout. Body man Dick Troutman, formerly the top body man at the Kurtis works, was assisted by

Charles Pelly in the design of this ultra-modern roadster. Frame man Tom Barnes, also from Kurtis, worked under the direction of Warren Olson, Reventlow's right-hand man. Emil Deidt, a leading West Coast body man who honed his talents with Harry Miller's famous Indy racers, was a key member of Reventlow's team. The driver for the team was Chuck Daigh, formerly of the Ford, Lincoln, Mercury, and Chevrolet racing teams, who did double duty as engine man and pilot. Jim Travers was shop superintendent, and Frank Coons specialized in engines. Travers and Coons were later to team up to form Traco, Chevrolet engine wizards extraordinaire. Troutman and Barnes had modified the HWM-Chevy and were also destined to become legends in auto racing. The Reventlow team's product was a stunningly beautiful, metallic blue roadster—one that reached extraordinary levels of performance.

The team started its project just after Labor Day 1957, and on January 16 the following year, the first Scarab was storming around the 2.5-mile Willow Springs track in its first tryouts, not yet with a body. Eight days later, the sleek roadster was out doing more laps, and drivers Daigh and Bruce Kessler lowered the track record by four seconds! On March 1 at Phoenix, Arizona's Beardsley Airport circuit, the Scarab's debut appearance was as a full-fledged racing car. The prototype had cost around $25,000—a bargain for what it became, but very expensive for the time. Kessler knocked several seconds off the

**(opposite)** The first Chevy V8 engine swap in a road racing car was in this HWM. It became the famed "Stovebolt Special," a formidable racing car in 1956.

**(below)** Vic Edelbrock was commissioned by car owner Bill Pollack to build the Chevrolet engine for his HWM.

A

B

existing record, and so did Richie Ginther, who lowered the track record with each successive lap to a best of 3.5 seconds under the record.

The Scarab name came from the lore of Egypt that said the scarab beetle was good luck and a sign of immortality. As time has told, Reventlow chose an appropriate name; the Scarab forged a legacy unmatched by American racing cars of its era. All of the cars he built have survived to this day.

Reventlow's crew designed and built three cars of the front engine/rear drive configuration in conformance with existing international regulations, and later built one rear engine sports racer that was also Chevrolet powered.

Reventlow's plan was to continue where Briggs Cunningham left off; that is, to try to break the tradition of European dominance on the race track. "I've got the chance of doing what most people only dream of doing," he once said. "I'm working toward the day when I can be in the same race with the top drivers of Europe, handling my own car, and beating them all fair and square. If and when that day comes, I'll know it's all been worthwhile." He planned to campaign the Scarabs in Europe on a full schedule, but the Continentals nixed those plans when they lowered the maximum acceptable engine displacement to three liters.

The Scarabs were excellent racing cars. In the beginning, the cars were fitted with Hilborn fuel-injected Corvette engines taken from 283 cubic inches to 302 CID (five liters). With 300 HP on tap, the 1,750-pound Scarab was formidable. Once the cars were put on the track, engine displacement went up

**(opposite)** The magnificent Scarab! Augie Pabst demonstrates the aluminum-bodied road racer, the Meister Bräuser, that he drove to win two national championships. Only three cars were built, two with right-hand drive.

**A.** Stark and functional, Scarab was the creation of Lance Reventlow, who financed the project with an inheritance received on his twenty-first birthday.

**B.** Chevrolet power from 1959. With Hilborn fuel injection, the Scarab set the trend for future Chevy-powered racing cars as seen in IMSA GTP twenty-five years later.

A

B

to 339 cubic inches. Tuned, equal length tubular headers joined thirty-two inches from exhaust ports into larger diameter side exhausts that released to the world the bellow of the Chevrolet V8. With a hotter cam, power was brought up to 390 HP at 7,000 RPM, but the final choice was a 270-degree design giving 375 BHP at 6,500 RPM.

The low-profile Hilborn FI system, using special angled ram tubes, gave a low hood profile so that the lines of the roadster were not spoiled with humps or bumps that would have resulted from using Chevrolet's own Rochester fuel injection. With gearing for 0-to-100 MPH in under nine seconds, and a top speed of more than 160 MPH, Scarabs simply laid waste to the opposition on American circuits in 1958. Scarabs also converted many builders from the old faithful 210 CID Jaguar inline-6 to the huge potential of the Chevrolet V8.

The first Scarab win was on June 1 at Santa Barbara. Reventlow simply walked away with the win. He proved it was no fluke when the team came to the east and Daigh won the Montgomery Nationals. Later in September at the United States Auto Club's (USAC) impressive 3.3-mile Meadowdale circuit near Chicago, Daigh and Reventlow trounced the normally invincible Lister-Jaguars with a one-two sweep.

Then, at USAC's Riverside Grand Prix, nearly one hundred thousand spectators saw Daigh post the quickest qualifying time of 2:04.03, a full two seconds under Phil Hill's 4.1-liter Ferrari. Reventlow was put out of the race when his Scarab was rammed by a Ferrari that split the car's fuel tank. The third car had been sidelined in practice, leaving Daigh to handle the howling pack alone. Daigh drove his Scarab to a tremendous victory over local greats including Bill

**(opposite) Devin SS was among the first successful "kit" type cars for the Chevrolet V8, although the complete car could be purchased. Only a few were built.**

**A. Tonneau covers looked good and provided additional aerodynamic benefits.**

**B. Stock Chevrolet V8s with a 4-BBL carburetor and 283 cubic inches delivered 220 HP at 4,800 RPM in 1957. Racing preparations easily added another 100.**

Pollack, Ken Miles, Richie Ginther, Dan Gurney, and Carroll Shelby, along with international stars of the highest caliber such as Phil Hill, Jean Behra, Roy Salvadori, Masten Gregory, Joachim Bonnier, and rising Indy drivers Jerry and Bobby Unser. Two hours, seventeen minutes after the green flag fell, after averaging 88.8 MPH for 203 miles, Daigh rolled in as the winner of the first USAC-FIA race held on the West Coast.

More wins followed in a stellar 1958 season that culminated in Nassau for Speed Week where Reventlow won the Bahamas Cup race and Daigh took the Nassau Trophy race, a clean sweep. Throughout the '58 season, the Scarab's Corvette four-speed transmissions gave no problems, proving the Chevrolet design more than capable of all-out racing. Inside, the two-seater was spacious, with full instrumentation behind the three-spoke, wood-rimmed steering wheel. But these appointments were pure function, designed for racing purposes; these were not GT cars for the street.

With a huge pile of victories over the best cars of the time, the Scarab inspired other Chevy V8-powered specials: Bocar, Echidna, Sadler, Lister-Corvette, and the Devin SS to name a few. Reventlow designed his sophisticated Scarabs to be full-bore racing cars, but the Devin SS became the first serious attempt at quantity manufacturing of a specialized Chevrolet V8-powered sports car for public sale.

Just how competitive the Devin SS body could become as a Chevy V8-powered sports-racer was shown by John Staver who won the SCCA B/Sports Racing National Championship in 1959. His car was homebuilt using as many 1956 Chevrolet junkyard parts as could be cleverly designed into a road racing car. Though not nearly as sophisticated as the Scarab, Staver's Echidna was just as formidable at

**(opposite) Bob Carnes's Bocar was another Chevy V8-powered road racer with formidable performance.**

**A. In the American tradition of left hand drive, the Bocar was both handsome and fast.**

**B. Chevrolet's 283 CID "small-block" with fuel injection was among the first production engines to achieve one horsepower per cubic inch.**

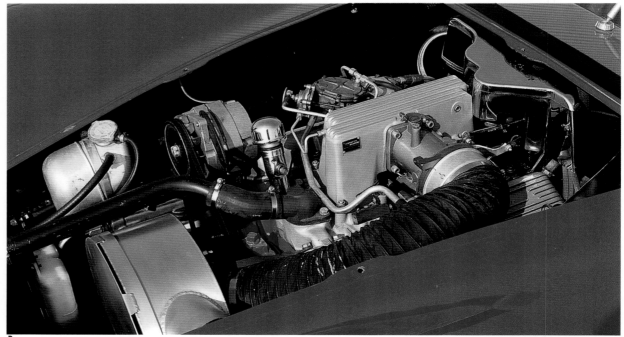

winning races. The name came from a favorite crossword puzzle word for the Australian spiny anteater, *echidna*. Such puzzles were entertainment during the long winter days in Minnesota, where Staver, Ed Grierson, and Bill Larson perpetuated the Echidna saga by building three of the cars that would carry them to numerous winner's circles—something that was not supposed to happen against the European cars of the time.

There were also some very highly developed Corvettes in the mid- to late-1950s, as was shown by Skip Hudson, who led a Corvette one-two-three sweep of the production sports car race at Riverside in 1959. His 81.7 MPH average victory showed just what Chevrolet's own sports car could do. Driving 'Vettes, Jim Jeffords of Milwaukee posted back-to-back SCCA national championships in B/Production in 1958 and '59. Everything Chevrolet's engineering team developed made its way to the racers. Corvette proved to be king of the hill in production class racing while the big-bore Chevy-powered modifieds took national championships. Augie Pabst took a record-setting title year as the 1959 USAC champion, then followed that victory by winning the 1960 SCCA title driving the awesome Meister Bräuser Scarabs.

The Automobile Manufacturers' Association (AMA) ban of 1957 held to by General Motors management did not allow factory involvement in racing, although experimental and styling work went on in hidden recesses of the corporation. One such styling experiment was built on Zora Arkus-Duntov's Corvette SS "mule" chassis built in 1957. The new car was ordered up by GM stylist Bill Mitchell and first ran in April 1959. This was the first Sting Ray, so named by Mitchell. His fascination with deep-sea creatures inspired his Sting Ray and Mako Shark.

Mitchell campaigned his Sting Ray as a private entry driven by Dr. Dick Thompson, the "flying dentist" from Washington, DC. The car won SCCA's C/Modified National Championship in 1960, the same year that Bob Johnson won the B/Production National championship in a Corvette. Mitchell's Sting Ray was the car that inspired the production Sting Ray introduced in 1963, the Corvette that became the great American dream machine.

Although a 1957 design, the front engine Scarab remained highly competitive through 1961 when Harry Heuer raced the Meister Bräusers, the cars owned by his father's brewery, to take the SCCA B/Sports Racing National Championship that year.

A primary competitor with the Chevy-powered sports-racers were the Jaguar-powered Lister specials. With the passing of the illustrious D-type Jaguar after its three Le Mans 24-Hours victories, Jaguars made little show in racing. However, proponents of the Jaguar marque championed a number of specials built around the famed inline 6-cylinder and four-speed gearbox. Until the arrival of the E-type in 1962, a number of builders adapted the Jaguar running gear to produce racing cars that were faster than the D-types largely because of lighter weight and more development. In England, the Lister-Jags driven by Archie Scott-Brown burst into racing with record-setting wins, and Jaguar was suddenly back. Although not true factory cars, fans claimed Lister-Jag victories as Jaguar wins just the same.

England's Brian Lister was the semi-official entry for factory racing in the late '50s. However promising his design was, Lister-Jaguar fans were stunned when the cars made their American debut at Sebring in 1958; the Lister-Jags were out of the running a little more than an hour into the twelve-hour enduro. The private entry D-types fared no better, and the days of production Jaguars in the winner's circle were eclipsed by Ferrari 250 GT cars.

Then, with the larger 3.8-liter engine Lister-Jag, Jaguar dealer Walt Hansgen of New York raced to victory at Marlboro, Maryland. The car proved to be an excellent racing car and was entered in every race conceivable. Hansgen had won the SCCA C/Modified National Championship in 1956, '57, and '58 in D-types. Some of his wins during the '58 season were in Alfred Momo's Lister-Jag, which Hansgen drove in the '59 season when he took that championship to make it four in a row.

Thompson won the 1960 C/Modified National Championship in Mitchell's Sting Ray and that inspired a new Lister special. Lister offered an alternative drive line with 1958 specifications: the Chevrolet small-block. This was essentially the

**(opposite)** "Echidna" was the name given to these Chevrolet-powered Devin SS-bodied road racing cars built on junk yard parts. They won a national championship!

**A.** Stark interiors were simple and functional.

**B.** When Chevrolet released its Rochester Fuel Injection system and four-speed transmission in 1957, the die was cast; Chevys were the racer's edge.

A

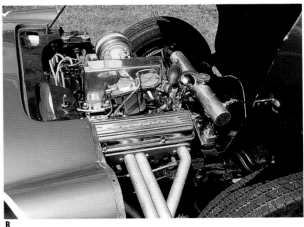

B

Corvette 283 with fuel injection and a four-speed transmission. The cars, known for their "knobbly" design because of the humps and bumps fashioned into the body to clear things underneath, were easily adapted to the Chevy engine. Rated at 290 HP at 6,200 RPM, the Lister-Corvette had 34 HP more than the Jag and was actually lighter. Weight distribution was nearly ideal, 48/52 front/rear. The slight rear bias made for sensational acceleration without spinning the tires. Gear ratios offered ranged from 2.93 to 4.78, giving the cars enormous versatility; they could run successfully on any track.

The Listers were designed for English sprint-type racing rather than long-distance endurance events, so they were naturals for American racing as well as European. Other than Sebring, few American races were longer than six hours.

Priced at $9,650, the Lister-Corvette was $700 cheaper than the Lister-Jag and offered more performance. Without an engine or transmission, buyers could acquire an otherwise complete Lister-Corvette for the attractive price of $6,604. For such an excellent racing car, that was a fair price indeed. The typical Ferrari cost more than $10,000 at the time and could not compete with either Jaguar- or Corvette-powered Listers. Peter Harrison showed the way to the winner's circle in SCCA racing by taking the 1961 C/Modified National Championship in a Lister-Corvette.

By this time, Chevrolet-powered sports-racing cars were firmly entrenched in American road racing. Harry Heuer continued the Chevy V8 dynasty in an improved Scarab, the Chaparral-1, designed and built by Troutman and Barnes. In the front engine Meister Bräuser Chaparral-1 cars, Heuer captured the SCCA C/Modified title in 1962 and '63.

**A.** Britain's Brian Lister established a legend with cars he built for the Jaguar inline-6 engine. When the "knobbly" received the Chevy V8, the car became faster and cheaper.

**B.** With 366 cubes of fuel-injected Chevy V8 cranking out 510 HP in 1964, the 1,500 pound Cheetah was a bullet.

**C.** The all-aluminum, lightweight Lister-Chevrolet was a formidable racing car that ran in Formula Libre races, similar to the later IMSA GT Prototype in concept.

A

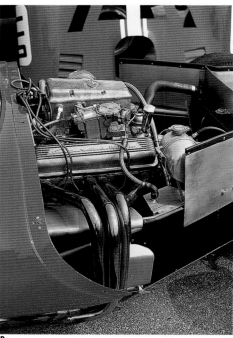
B

C

A

A. "Awesome!" describes the Cheetah well. The combination of light weight and over 200 MPH speeds with missile-like acceleration clearly showed the way for racing Chevy V8s.

B. The rear engine revolution eclipsed front engine racing cars with better handling and quicker lap times. The Cooper-Chevrolet of 1964 was among the first professional class road racing cars of this type.

C. The Cooper-Chevrolet demonstrated all the features seen in IMSA GT Prototype cars twenty years later.

B

C

A

A. The Lola T-70 began the long tradition of Eric Broadley's marque. This is the Roger Penske/Mark Donohue Sunoco Special of 1967, the year Donohue won the USRRC.

B. Although markedly different in appearance, the later Lola T-600 and T-710 cars were actually extensive developments of the T-70 with a ground effect coupe body.

C. The aluminum tub, power train, and chassis layout of the T-70 laid the foundation for a generation of Chevrolet-powered prototype cars, including the GTP cars, whose designs incorporated newer and stronger materials.

D. New Zealander, Bruce McLaren, began his own tradition of winning road races with the Chevrolet-powered M6 McLarens he drove to the SCCA Can-Am Challenge Cup Championship in 1967.

E. McLaren's works cars raced the Can-Am to a second championship in 1968 driven by Denny Hulme. Chevrolet power dominated American professional class racing.

F. With an 8.1-liter (494 CID) Chevy big-block engine, the 740 HP McLaren M8F of 1971 was eclipsed the next year by Porsche's entry into the Can-Am with turbocharged 5.4-liter cars with 1,040 HP. That began the turbo era.

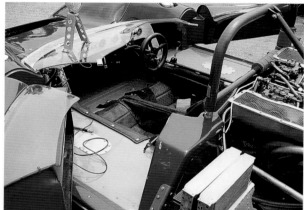

B

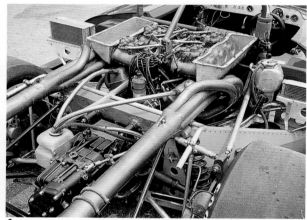

C

D

E

F

The successes of Chevy V8 power in road racing inspired other builders to produce their own versions of high-powered street/racing cars. One such builder was California's Bill Thomas, whose Cheetah was a truly astounding performer, one of the quickest front engine cars ever built. Bob Carnes of Denver entered his Bocar in the highly competitive field, as did Bill Devin with his turn-key Devin SS.

By the early 1960s, racing car design was rapidly changing. Front engine cars were no longer competitive as rear engine designs swept victory after victory. By moving the Chevy V8 behind the driver, a new evolution of American V8-powered European racing cars emerged. One was the Cooper-Chevy; essentially a British-designed and -built Cooper-Monaco with the four-banger yanked out and a small-block V8 stuffed in its place. Roger Penske took three consecutive SCCA D/Modified National Championships in small engine Coopers. By 1964 a professional racing series emerged, the United States Road Racing Championship (USRRC), followed by the Can-Am in 1966.

The concept of the rear engine racing car led to Eric Broadley's Lola T-70 in which Mark Donohue won two consecutive USRRC titles in 1967 and '68 with Penske's Sunoco Special Lola. Similar cars designed and built by Bob McKee also raced successfully; one was co-driven by Dick Smothers of the Smothers Brothers comedy team. There was Jim Hall's Chaparral-2 cars in which he won the 1964 USRRC. And Bruce McLaren's soon-to-be unbeatable McLaren specials were successfully handled by Chuck Parsons, who won the USRRC title in a McLaren-Chevrolet in 1966. From 1967 through 1970, McLaren and Denny Hulme took alternate Can-Am titles in successively faster McLarens, completely dominating their sport.

By 1960, front engine Chevrolet-powered sports cars dominated road racing throughout America. By 1970, big-block Chevy V8s behind the driver had taken their place. And by 1980, a new generation of Chevy-powered road racers emerged to end Porsche's stranglehold on IMSA road racing. Enter Brian Redman and the Cooke-Woods Lola T-600, another Chevy V8-powered racing car that became champion in its debut season (1981). Following that auspicious year, the Corvette GTP stood poised to continue the Chevrolet legacy.

**A.** Brian Redman, one of the world's premier drivers, has won on most of the world's major road racing tracks and emerged victorious in championships with 2-liter to 5-liter cars. He has won many races in open wheel and full body cars, and was team driver with Ford, Porsche, Ferrari, and Chevron in five World Championships. He also invented the modern IMSA GTP concept with this car, the Cooke-Woods Lola T-600, that took him to another championship.

**B.** With five victories and five seconds in ten starts, Redman won the 1981 IMSA championship in the Cooke-Woods Lola-Chevrolet, the car he inspired. He could drive anything to victory, and changed the course of IMSA GT racing.

**C.** The mid-mounted Chevrolet V8 with "bundle of snakes" tubular exhausts and fuel injection was very similar to the Lola T-70 of 1966, but extensively modernized and fitted with a ground effect body.

**D.** Porsche's 935 Turbo was a 750 HP dual turbocharged flat-6 that won World Championships in 1976, '77, '78, and '79. It won the 24-Hours of Le Mans in 1979 and dominated IMSA GT Prototype racing as well.

**E.** Many 935 Turbo teams were prominent during the years around 1980. The Bayside Disposal entries with Bruce Levin and Hurley Haywood were always tough to beat.

D

E

## Lola T-600

The new era of Chevrolet power in top-rank American road racing began when the Lola T-600 ground effect coupe first raced at Laguna Seca, California, on May 3, 1981. The car was so radical in styling that it caught everyone's attention. The typical sports-racer of the time was the Porsche 935, a derivative of the aged 911 of the mid-1960s. The Cooke-Woods Racing Lola was dramatically new among the established European cars. With its rear fender skirts, ground effects, and—of all things—a fuel-injected Chevrolet small-block V8, the car evoked guffaws from fans who thought the turbocharged Porsches were invincible. The guffaws were quickly silenced.

An iron block Chevrolet V8 going up against the big boys? For those who remembered the Scarabs, the T-70s, the Can-Am McLarens, and the Formula 5000 cars, there was no doubt that Chevrolet's engine could beat Porsche. But the bright yellow Cooke-Woods Lola was so new, with no development time, that it was initially seen as just another wild attempt to unseat the well-proven Porsche Turbos. To vanquish an all-conquering car like the IMSA GTX-class 935 meant a David and Goliath match-up; it looked like a hopeless task.

In qualifying for that first race, the Porsche Turbos were quicker; four of them were in the hands of top drivers. Championship driver Brian Redman suited up to drive the Cooke-Woods Lola and was uncharacteristically nervous. He was driving the new car, but it was more than just a new car. If this car failed to win this race, Eric Broadley and his time-honored Lola works would collapse in financial ruin. Redman had read IMSA's GTP regulations and recognized that a radical and inventive car with Chevrolet V8 power could beat the Porsches. But being radical and inventive was very difficult and costly. Broadley had spent a good portion of his career stepping beyond the norm, but the T-600 pushed the envelope. Would the car's ground effects work? Would it stay together during the grueling sprints where success or failure often hinged on a few seconds? Redman strapped himself into the car knowing that success would be glorious, as it always is in racing, but failure would become no more than a footnote in the history of racing car oddities.

An illustrious driver ranked among the very best that racing has ever produced, Redman knew what was at stake. He had driven for many of the world's best racing teams, teams that raced only fully developed cars with proper preparation and support. Only with these elements could a team—such as John Wyer's Gulf-Porsche team that won two World Championships with full Porsche factory backing—hope to be competitive, much less win championships. Redman gripped the wheel of the only T-600 in existence for its debut appearance. With little development time and without a major team effort behind him, his entry onto the starting grid at Laguna Seca was literally for all the marbles. Could he, an experienced driver with a sterling career, have misjudged the challenge of introducing a new car against the thoroughbreds?

He had been on six successive world championship teams, won sixteen endurance races on the top tracks of the world (including Daytona and Sebring), won the first 2-liter World Championship as well, and become *the* driver in 5-liter-powered Formula 5000 racing for three successive years. With that kind of experience, why should he be nervous about another race?

Everything was on the line. To finish was not enough. To place was not enough. He had to win. The Lola T-600 had taken so much of Broadley's resources that if it did not win at Laguna Seca, Lola would be broke.

Redman positioned the car a conservative fifth on the starting grid. Klaus Ludwig in the Team Miller Mustang Turbo, the official Ford Motor Company entry, was gridded fourth. John Fitzpatrick had the pole in a Porsche 935 Turbo, having set a record qualifying lap of 1:01.54 at an average speed of 111.145 MPH over the challenging 1.9-mile Laguna Seca course. John Paul, Jr. held the second position in another Porsche Turbo. Rising Indy star Bobby Rahal was gridded third in yet another Porsche Turbo. David Hobbs held the seventh position in the factory-backed BMW M-1/C racing in GTP class. Al Unser, Jr. piloted a GTO M-1 starting eighteenth.

One of IMSA's all-time leading winners, Hurley Haywood, piloted still another Porsche Turbo gridded ninth.

Of the thirty-nine starters in the race, eleven of the cars were well-proven Porsche Turbos driven by thoroughly experienced drivers. As expected, at the finish of fifty-three laps, four of the top five cars were Porsche Turbos. Against overwhelming odds, Redman brought his lone Lola T-600 in victorious, setting a race lap record of 1:03.02. At an average speed of 108.537 MPH, he and the new car had performed a miracle and ended the Porsche dynasty with the car's debut victory. It was an historic moment.

Suddenly the Porsche 935s had a master, but they were still highly competitive. As the season progressed and Redman dialed in the Lola further, it became the fastest, best-handling car that IMSA racing had ever seen. He won the championship that year by a huge margin despite entering the fray in the fifth race of the season.

Redman drove the car to victory in the next two races, Lime Rock and Mid-Ohio, then did not enter the Lola at Brainerd, the following race, where Ludwig bested the Porsches in the Team Miller Mustang. The Cooke-Woods entry also bypassed the six-hour at Daytona in early July, which Haywood and Mauriceo DeNaraez won in a Porsche Turbo. At Sears Point on July 26, John Paul, Jr. handled the third Lola T-600 built and set a qualifying lap record of 1:33.56 at 97.081 MPH. He went on to set a race record lap of 1:40.71, but Ludwig won again, ahead of Redman's second place. Paul finished third. At Portland on August 2, Paul once again showed the superiority of the Lola T-600 by setting the pole and fastest race lap, but Redman walked away with the win by one minute and thirty-three seconds over Porsche Turbos in at second and third. Paul set a blistering pace, but Redman's cool, calculating patience as a precision driver, which accounted for more racing victories than his younger competitors had years, led to his fourth checkered flag of the season.

The next race was a 1,000-kilometer enduro at Mosport, Canada, in which the Porsche Turbos set

the pole and fastest lap. Redman started thirty-fifth, last on the grid, then blasted around seventeen cars on the first lap! It wasn't long before he was dueling with Paul's T-600 and Rolf Stommelen's 935 Turbo for the lead. When the hard-charging Paul ended up in the catch net, Stommelen and Redman went on to finish in that order.

Stommelen succeeded in winning the following race at Road America ahead of Redman with Chris Cord and Jim Adams in at third in the fourth T-600 built. Redman was not in the August 30 race at Mid-Ohio, and both Paul's and Cord's T-600s fared poorly, finishing near the bottom of the roster.

As the 1981 IMSA Camel GT season wound its way south to Road Atlanta, no driver had emerged yet as champion, and everyone at the race was filled with anticipation. Several drivers had a shot at the title if Redman did not fare well. With only three races remaining, Redman needed this victory to win the championship. In a rare coincidence, Redman pitted for fuel just as a car crashed and burned. The race stopped, and his fourth placing instantly improved on the restart as he joined the field right behind the leaders, who had yet to pit. Paul made a blinding dash race of it to the end, showing the capability of the T-600 at the very limit, but was unable to regain the lead. As the only driver on the lead lap, Redman won the race and clinched the IMSA Drivers Championship, a first for a British driver and British car. This feat won great admiration from the fans and racers alike.

The season was not over for Redman or Lola. The team of John Paul, Jr. and John Paul, Sr. won the next race at Pocono in a rain-shortened event in which their Sachs-sponsored Porsche 935 swapped the lead with the Redman/Ralph Kent Cooke and Chris Cord/Jim Adams Lola T-600 teams eleven times. With a two-minute lead when the rain came, the Pauls were victorious in a furious battle in which the Cooke-Woods Lola finished second.

In the final race that decided national championships in most classes, the Daytona high-bank and infield road course featured seventy-two cars. John Fitzpatrick set the pole and the race fastest lap in his Porsche Turbo. The lead changed seven times

A

A. Peter Gregg's Brumos Porsche 935 Turbo leads the pack at Daytona where he won the 24-Hours four times. This is the car that he raced to win the 1979 IMSA Championship.

B.The Lee Racing Corvette GTP of Lew Price was the first of the Lola T-710 series cars to race the Daytona 24-Hours of 1985. Lew Price, Carson Baird, and Terry Labonte drove from thirteenth at the start, but did not finish.

C. Don Whittington won the March-Chevrolet's first GTP race of 1984 at Road Atlanta. Randy Lanier won three in a row at Riverside, Laguna Seca, and Charlotte, then won at Portland, Michigan, and Watkins Glen to take the IMSA GTP championship in this March-Chevrolet.

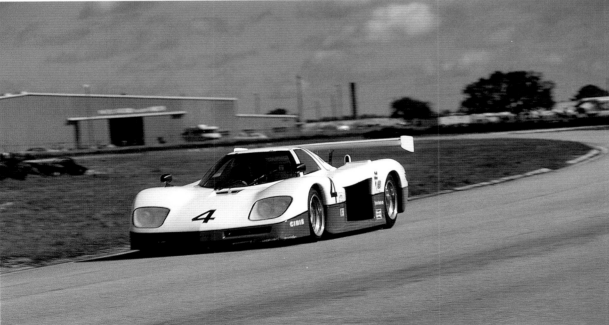

B

C

A

A. GTP in 1984 brought together the broadest variety of cars yet seen in IMSA racing and pitted normally aspirated cars against increasing numbers of turbo cars, mainly Porsches. This is the 1984 IMSA champion, Randy Lanier, and his 84G March-Chevrolet V8. Like Redman's Lola T-600, Lanier's March broke Porsche's eleven-year stranglehold on the IMSA championship.

B. In 1985, the remarkable Löwenbräu Special Porsches took both the IMSA Championship and the World Endurance Championship.

B

between Redman's Lola and the Porsche Turbos of John Paul, Jr. and Fitzpatrick. It was a thrilling race as the drivers diced between themselves and unexpected events such as the failure of the turbo on Fitzpatrick's Porsche and an unexpected pit stop by Redman.

With Paul leading and Redman closing, the Lola displayed superiority to the Porsches by regaining lost time and moving out front with ten laps remaining. Running smoothly to the flag and several seconds in the lead on the last lap, a back marker erupted in smoke just as Redman moved up to pass on the last lap and the checkered flag. He backed off, but Paul didn't, and Paul's Porsche flashed through the smoke to take the win with Redman finishing second.

Porsche locked up the Manufacturers Championship, but Redman was the new IMSA Driver Champion. His six wins, five in the Lola, along with his victory in the first race of the season (Daytona with Bobby Rahal and Bob Garretson while driving a Porsche Turbo) netted Redman the title with 213 points to 130 for Paul (who would win the IMSA title the next year) and 111 points for Fitzpatrick (the 1980 IMSA Champion). Porsches won nine of the sixteen races, and Mustangs won two.

The level of difficulty in challenging the Porsches and the awesome accomplishment of becoming a giant killer shows in the Mustang record. With full factory support and years of development by the highly successful Zakspeed team, veteran driver and German champion Klaus Ludwig raced in seven races, but won only two and placed second once. Ill luck and an assortment of problems continually thwarted the Mustang effort. Redman's completely independent Cooke-Woods Lola raced in ten races, winning five times and coming in second five times. No one, except Redman, imagined such a success at the beginning of the season. He won more than $107,000 for his efforts.

The 1981 IMSA GTP season was truly remarkable; an entirely new entry vanquished the horde of Porsche Turbos and opened the door to a new era of IMSA racing. The success of the Cooke-Woods Lola reflected its superb preparation, a credit to successful racer John Bright, who had encountered personal tragedy in England and set his sights on America and new racing opportunities. Redman suggested he stay on, build the car at Lola, and bring it to the United States for the IMSA GTP season. Bright became chief mechanic and engineer of the Cooke-Woods Lola. Redman credited much of his superlative record to Bright's preparation.

Later, Bright was involved with the Chevrolet-powered Lola T-610, the intermediary between the T-600 and the GM Goodwrench T-710. The T-610 languished in development, waiting for GM to make financial commitments to racing. The development team tested the car at Laguna Seca with Mario Andretti, Al Unser, Sr., and Al Unser, Jr., all of whom showed the car to be incredibly quick, but GM motorsports officials were undecided about what was to come next. No sponsorship meant no team. Bright returned to Lola to work on Formula One cars and the Lola-Chevrolet went under wraps.

A few people at Chevrolet had noted the success of the T-600 and regarded the T-610 as the next logical step toward a competitive racing car, but it would be 1983 before the factory made an acknowledged return to racing. But that re-entry was into NASCAR with the new Monte Carlo. However, the success of the Lola T-600 fed long-held ambitions of a world-class road racing Chevrolet.

The Cooke-Woods Lola was a radical and highly successful GTP car. The first T-600 was chassis number HU-1 and was the first coupe Broadley had built since the T-70 Mk IIIB and T-163 lines of the 1960s. The new car eclipsed Porsche and the GTO Division BMW M-1 to establish Chevrolet power as a new force in GTP racing. The Lolas sent competing designers and engineers back to their drawing boards, computers, and wind tunnels to invent a new generation of prototypes. As a result, competition in America's top road racing series escalated dramatically, and Chevrolet-powered cars were a major force in 1982 and '83, but the Goodwrench Corvette GTP was another year or so away. During those years, chassis builders lined up with their versions of the T-600 concept, usually powered by American V8 engines, and the European factories came back with their new cars, quicker and faster than ever. There was Porsche with its new 962 and, in a few years, BMW moved up to GTP with a new car.

From Britain came another chassis builder in the Lola tradition, March Racing, whose cars ran in all sorts of racing series including the Indianapolis 500, Formula One, and the World Endurance Championship (WEC). The 82G chassis with Chevrolet power emerged a front challenger during the 12-Hours of Sebring in 1982 when the Bobby Rahal/Jim Trueman/Mauriceo DeNaraez team finished second overall, within two minutes of the winner. The winning Porsche 935, driven by the father and son team of John Paul, Sr. and John Paul, Jr., narrowly missed being eclipsed by the March-Chevrolet.

Randy Lanier's Blue Thunder March-Chevy finished second overall at Sebring in 1984, and by then the March chassis powered by Chevy's powerful V8 had emerged as the dominant car in IMSA GTP. Lanier won the championship that year in a pair of Blue Thunder Racing entries, both 350 CID Chevrolet V8-powered March 84G cars. His six victories were backed up by team driver Bill Whittington, who set twelve new records. Lanier and Whittington finished one-two in the IMSA point race that year ahead of Al Holbert and Derek Bell, who finished third and fourth driving the new Porsche 962.

The March chassis could also be fitted with a Porsche engine similar to the 962, and Andial was the source of the power plants in this country. The March-Porsche sponsored by Kreepy Krauly, a South African manufacturer of swimming pool cleaners, won the first round of the 1984 season. Team manager, Ken Howes, and lead driver, Sarel Van Der Merwe, were from South Africa and would later figure strongly in the Corvette GTP effort. Kreepy Krauly won the first round of the 1984 season, the 24-Hours of Daytona, and launched careers in American racing that would take them to the Corvette GTP the next year. The March chassis was as comfortable with the Chevrolet V8 as the Porsche flat-six.

In the race at Daytona, Redman was in the latest GTP Jaguar, the XJR-5, driving the second of two Bob Tullius-prepared Group 44 Jags. He set the

fastest lap of the race, a new track record (1:57.36 at 118.987 MPH), but on the pole was a new Andial-powered Porsche. The 962 was driven by ace drivers Mario and Mike Andretti. Mario Andretti set the fastest qualifying lap, also a new record at 1:50.99 (at an average speed of 125.526 MPH), but the car lasted only 127 laps. That season, Al Holbert in the Löwenbräu Porsche 962 won five races, but failed to repeat his IMSA Championship of the previous year and was beaten by Lanier's Blue Thunder March-Chevy.

Van Der Merwe and Kreepy Krauly won again at Lime Rock, another fine victory, beating Lanier's similar March-Chevrolet and Holbert's Porsche 962. In the next race at Mid-Ohio on June 10, Holbert and Derek Bell took the 962's first victory, leading the Lanier/Whittington March-Chevy at the finish. That same year, a pair of front engine Mustang GTP cars, Ford's latest effort with in-house designed and fabricated carbon fiber chassis racing cars, showed speed, but—as expected—lacked stamina.

The Mustang GTP was a completely new racing car, designed from the ground up, that drew deeply on Ford's ultra-high technology aerospace, manufacturing, and motorsports capabilities. Against the stock block Chevy-powered GTP cars and the new Porsche 962 running the venerable turbocharged flat-six, the Ford cars came up rather short even though they showed good form with pole positions and two wins.

The Mustang GTP team earned great satisfaction with a debut victory on August 31, 1983, at Road America, where they overcame a strong field of Porsches, Marches, Lolas, and Jaguars to finish first and third. It was the first time an American driver (Rahal) had won a major international race in an American-built car entered by a major manufacturer. The Turbo-4-powered Mustang GTP was an official Ford Motor Company entry, and paved the way for Chevrolet to return to racing, although GM preferred to do battle by purchasing a chassis from Lola rather than building its own.

The Ford team only ran three races in 1983, and results were not as promising as the team had hoped. However, winning one race at Road America

after being just 0.2 seconds off the pole proved that the Ford engineers were on the right track.

During the 1984 season, competition toughened, and Ludwig finished no higher than fifth (Sears Point and Daytona) with more powerful Fords running 2.1-liter rather than 1.7-liter engines. At Laguna Seca, for example, Ludwig and Bob Wollek drove these front engine, 600 HP (at 9,000 RPM) cars to finish twelfth and thirteenth against cars with 6- and 8-cylinder engines exceeding 700 HP.

During that season, another new car appeared, the Ford-Argo. With the legendary Ford Cosworth V8 behind the driver, the Ford-Argo driven by Lyn St. James ran a smooth race to finish tenth at Laguna Seca on May 6. St. James finished the highest of any Ford driver that season, finishing third overall behind two March-Chevys at Watkins Glen on September 30 while on the same lap as the leaders. Her car was not the first Ford-Argo on the tracks that year. Don Courtney and Brent O'Neill raced their Ford-Argo in several races beginning with the second round at Miami (finishing nineteenth overall, not running).

These cars, with well-established Ford-Cosworth engines with displacement from 3.0- to 3.7-liters, revealed the difficulties every team faced when introducing a new car. Even with deep technological support, victory lane proved elusive for the Ford drivers, while the teams running Chevrolet V8 engines, led by Lanier in the Blue Thunder March-Chevrolet, won another championship. While the Ford team fought interminable bad luck, the March-Chevrolet successes piled up, largely through the efforts of independent teams. It was a frustrating year for the Ford team, which further illustrates the significance of the success of other debut cars: Redman's astounding championship in the Lola T-600 during 1981 and Lanier's superb season in 1984.

During the 1984 season, Chevrolet racked up 248 points to best Porsche's 246 and win the GTP Engine Manufacturer Championship. The GTP Chassis Manufacturer Championship was taken by March, which had 263 points to Porsche's 224. Jaguar was a distant third in both tallies with 144 points. Ford amassed only 75 engine points and 16 chassis points, despite race leads and pole wins

by Ludwig, Rahal, and Wollek, and impressive driving by St. James.

The new Jaguars, Porsches, March cars, and a host of other top competitors made the 1984 IMSA GTP the most exciting racing anywhere. With 136 new records set during the season, it was an historic year for GTP racing. Bill Whittington, in the Blue Thunder March-Chevrolet, set seven new qualifying records—four in consecutive races. He set two new race records and won three races at record speeds. However, the venerable Porsche 935 was still a capable car, as shown by the Joest Racing entry that whipped the best GTP entries at Sebring by winning with a two-lap margin over the Blue Thunder March-Chevy.

By winning seven of sixteen races that year, Chevrolet was still the force to contend with in GTP racing. When Holbert and Bell rolled the Löwenbräu Special Porsche into the winner's circle at Mid-Ohio, they showed that the German engineers had learned quickly. When faced with the Chevrolet-powered cars, they introduced a radical new Porsche for the purpose of recapturing the IMSA crown and for introducing a new contender in WEC racing, the 962. The previous dominance of the 935 in IMSA GTX class was based on extensive modifications to production cars. Like the Jaguar XJR-5, the new GTP Porsche was strictly a prototype, a purpose-built car with no production connections except the engine, as derived from the Type 911 flat-six, which was similar to the 935. The Jag engine was based on the production V12 and ran normally aspirated.

With that first victory, the new Porsche began a succession of fifty wins spanning the period of time that the Corvette GTP was in its prime. The 962 proved to be a highly competitive car that dominated GTP racing as thoroughly as the 935s had done in the years before Brian Redman's Cooke-Woods Lola T-600 changed IMSA racing.

**(opposite) Sarel Van Der Merwe and Crew Chief Ken Howes made believers of IMSA racing at Daytona and Lime Rock in 1984 with this March-Porsche.**

A

A. Ford's space age Mustang GTP was a 1,770-pound rocket capable of 210-plus MPH. In its debut race, the two-car team won at Elkhart Lake (1983) with a one-two sweep.

B. The Klaus Ludwig/Tim Coconis Ford GTP led the Bobby Rahal/Geoff Brabham team car into victory lane with a record win.

B

A

B

A. The Group 44 Jags finished two-three at Charlotte in 1984. Note the trailing Cosworth V8 Ford-Argo, also known as the C-100 in European racing, where it was also unsuccessful.

B. Bob Tullius's beautiful Group 44 cars received a lot of press and were capable of winning anywhere. Tullius set fastest lap at Miami, and Bundy set fastest lap at Road Atlanta, a track record, in this car.

manifold that became the popular standard wear for Formula 5000. Then, of course, development on the engines went ahead slowly, as it always has done. You know you gain a little bit here and there. The engine builders would work on the engines and would get a bit more bottom end power, a bit more top end power, a bit more revs. You know, just as usual.

The engines were eventually 8,000 RPM engines and very strong. We had tremendous reliability from our Chaparral F-5000 engines built by Franz Weis. He was Jim Hall's engine builder and chief mechanic and chief car tester. He was a very good driver and a wonderful engine builder. He is one of the best engine builders in the country. We had immense reliability at the time when Chevys really weren't so reliable. We ran four years with Formula 5000, winning three championships, and we had one engine failure in that time. The T-70s with the Chevrolet engine were cast iron, and the 5000s were also.

There were differences in weight—five hundred pounds difference between the Lola T-70 and a Formula 5000 car. So that in itself makes everything different. I didn't really take so much notice as to what was actually being done to the engines, and they certainly didn't tell me very much. Engine building is a bit of a magic art, and the builders don't share the secrets, do they?

In 1968 I came to the States, but it was 1973 before I ran regularly in North America. I came to the States in 1972 with my own car, a Chevron, to do some Formula 5000 events, and we finished second in the championship that year to Jody Scheckter, who became Formula One World Champion. We missed three races because I was driving for Ferrari in Europe in the endurance events, and we missed the Formula 5000 championship by only a few points. I think we won five out of the eight races, so we won most of the races that we ran in; we just didn't do enough races. The total points weren't high enough. I went on to win the championship in 1974, '75, and '76.

In 1972, I was driving Formula 5000 in Europe and three races in America. I was also driving for the McLaren team in an M19 McLaren, standing in when Peter Revson was busy doing American races. When he was doing Indianapolis and some of the other big Indy car events, I drove instead of him in the McLaren Formula One teams. So I had almost a direct comparison of F-5000 and F-1 on a week-by-week basis.

The Formula One car was lighter, and its power band was narrower. You had to work with the gearbox much more than in the 5000. The Formula One car braked a bit better because it was lighter, and it was a bit better balanced, but it didn't have the power coming out of the corners. So the actual difference in lap times between the Formula One and the Formula 5000 was almost nothing. Sometimes the 5000s were actually faster than the Formula One cars. There wasn't much difference. Formula 5000 became the national formula all over the world, really. It was in South Africa, New Zealand, Australia, America, and England.

It didn't replace Formula One; it was in addition to Formula One. Several races, both in America and in Europe, were combined events—not the world championship races, the non-championship events. In fact, Formula 5000 cars did win some of those combined events. And Skip Barber had a Formula One March in the Formula 5000 series. They were allowed in. There were races where the 5000s raced against the Formula One cars.

The main reason for Formula 5000 was it used low cost, powerful racing cars. It seems crazy when you think about it now. The engines were much less expensive than the Cosworth engines and easier to maintain. Otherwise, the cars were quite similar. It was just a cheaper formula of a very powerful racing car.

I had a horrendous crash testing a full-body Formula 5000 car—a Can-Am car, really—at St. Jovite, Canada, in 1977. The Sports Car Club of America planned to call these full-bodied cars Can-Am cars in hopes of reviving interest in the series. The car was light in the front, and just a bit before I turned over, Elliott Forbes-Robinson did the same thing in the same place, but he landed on his wheels. He did a complete loop. I only did half a loop. I went about thirty feet in the air at 170 miles per hour, and came down upside down.

During the period after the crash, while recovering from my extensive injuries, I raced off and on. Racing in those days wasn't like today. There wasn't much money. I was doing five or six races a year at that point, still living in England. And not having any business in England, that was my sole income.

I was really helped by Jo Hoppen, who was the competition manager for VW-Porsche-Audi. He helped me a lot by providing me with rides. He would find me a car, and he would pay me to drive.

By 1979, it was obvious that I really had to do something. This was about two years after the accident, so I talked to Carl Haas, the US Lola importer, and having driven for him for four years, he was a friend of mine. He said if I would like to come and sell racing cars, come on over. So in 1980, we moved to Lake Forest in Illinois, and I went to work as a racing car salesman.

At about that time we had received the IMSA rules for GTP cars, and also at that time, I think that Porsche had lost only one race in four years in IMSA. John Bishop, IMSA's director, quite rightly, was very anxious to change that. He wanted competition. He wrote a set of rules which kind of favored the Chevrolet engine. I read the rules, and I said to Carl that Lola could build a car that could probably win races under these rules. He agreed.

I had to go to England anyway, to see Eric Broadley on some other business things, and I took the rules to Eric and told him, "Eric, you could build a car that fit these rules." He said, "Yes, we could." So I went back to Carl and told him that Eric agreed. "Can we order two cars?" Carl said, "No. I am not buying them."

They were $80,000 each, without the engines, and Eric needed the money up front for those orders before he could build a car. That was in 1980. Carl told me that if I could find someone to buy the cars, then he would split the profit on sales of future models and on parts. He is the sole importer for Lola, so any car made by Lola must come through Carl. I was friendly with Roy Woods, who I had known from the Formula 5000 days when he was entrant of the Carling Black Label car. He was an owner, but he was also a driver. He was a good driver who had also driven in the Trans-Am. He showed some signs of interest in the GTP, and so did Ralph Cooke. He and Roy decided to form a partnership and buy the first two cars. The project started to go ahead in July or August of 1980.

Ralph and Roy were going to have a big team that would also have Trans-Am cars that they would drive and incorporate Can-Am cars that Carl Haas would enter and the Lola T-600 that I would have in the IMSA Camel GT series. So, on one of my trips to England, Carl said, "Why don't you meet with this guy John Bright, who sent a letter looking for employment." I met with John at Lola. We got on together right away, and he said, "I would like to move to America right away, and yes, I would love to look after building this car." So, my instruction to him was to build it and have it in America by the end of March, come what may, of 1981, whatever Eric said. "It has to be in America by the end of March!" He really spearheaded that, and built both of the cars and sent them out.

The engines were done by Chaparral, who, at that time, had a new engine builder, Gerald Davis. He had taken over for Franz Weis because Weis had joined VDS Racing, and that is still what his shop is called today. VDS Racing was formed in partnership with Count Van Der Straten, who was a great racing enthusiast and supported Formula 5000 and other cars for many years. He built a shop in Midland, Texas, and Franz was a part owner of it.

Franz had worked for Jim Hall for many years back in the old Chaparral days. When they came to Europe, he was one of the mechanics. He is from Stuttgart in Germany and is just a great mechanic. He left, and so Gerald Davis, who had been a sprint car engine builder, joined Chaparral Cars, and he built our engines. And again, they were great engines, 350-cubic-inch Chevrolets.

We weren't allowed to use aluminum heads at that time. Later on, we did use them when IMSA changed their minds. We had the time when we could use Brodix heads, then we couldn't use Brodix heads. It was a big confusion. But again we had great performance from these Gerald Davis/Chaparral engines. We only had one engine for a

long time. We would fly it back and forth. John Bright would take it out of the car on Monday after the race, fly it to Midland, Texas, and we would have it on Thursday. It went to Midland for overhaul and back to us for the next race.

The first race for this new car in the IMSA series was very important. We tested it at Sears Point in April of 1981, and we knew it was good right away because we were close on the lap times of the records held by Danny Ongais in the Interscope Porsche 935. We took it to Riverside a week later. We ran it around Riverside and again the times were good. We had some problems with the cars but nothing really drastic. It was basically a good car.

The T-600 had no real relationship to the T-70. At one time, though, it had been seriously discussed that we would build a more modern version of the T-70, but Eric said, "No, it is not the right way to do it. We should build a ground effects car along current technology lines."

It was basically Eric who suggested ground effects. But, of course, ground effects were the big thing at that time. So when the opportunity arose and the rules didn't ban ground effects, it was the thing that we obviously had to do because ground effects were already proven in Formula One. It was taking Formula One ground effects and modifying it to sports cars. Quite a lot of work was done in the wind tunnel by Lola, and the car came with full ground effects.

It was the ace for the early days for ground effects in relation to sports cars. We knew how good it was when we had good road holding and good braking, but the car had a diving about under braking problem. It had something to do with the suspension layout, we think, and we never really found out what it was. But the car, otherwise, was very good right away. The balance was good and we could change it by altering the wing or the roll bars. We had a very well-balanced car.

We could have run it first in the Riverside six hours, but we thought that was really the wrong place for a new car. We didn't know how long the engine would run. We didn't know what the life of the engine would be, so we decided to run it at the one-

hour Laguna Seca meeting in May of 1981. 'Course, everyone came for the race; Eric Broadley was there, Carl Haas, Ralph Cooke, Roy Woods, everybody.

I was a nervous wreck. I was responsible not only for driving it, but I was organizing the team as well, team manager and driver. The night before the race, Carl takes a big draw on his cigar, blows out a cloud of smoke, and says to me, "You realize, if this car doesn't win, it could bankrupt Lola."

I was an absolute ruin. I hadn't slept for days. I didn't qualify very well, I was about fifth. The race started and I immediately dropped back to about eighth because the car felt very bad going into Turn 2. Turn 2 at Laguna Seca is one of the most difficult turns in all of North American road racing. It is just about flat-out, or was in those days, and when I came off the power for just an instant going into Turn 2, the car was moving around. There was something wrong with it. It hadn't been doing that in practice.

The first thing that you think of is a tire going bad or a loose wheel, and every single lap I said to myself, "I have got to go in the pits." But I knew if I did there was no chance of success because in a one-hour race, you can't make a pit stop. I kept going and on about the tenth lap it was OK, so I started moving up, and eventually I won the race. I moved to the front at probably three-quarters of the way through.

After the race, we found that the left rear wheel nut had worked loose, backed up against the spring steel safety retainer, breaking it off, and wound itself back on again. Someone was looking after us!

I had a big run with John Paul, Jr. in his 935 Porsche, and with Bobby Rahal, who was in our team 935. Bobby and I had just won the Daytona 24-Hours together, in the Cooke-Woods 935 Porsche, prepared by Garretson Engineering.

The Cooke-Woods Lola T-600 was a very, very good car. ➤

# Origin of the Corvette GTP

The Lola T-600 and March-Chevrolets were so influential that they spawned great enthusiasm among Chevrolet racing fans everywhere. The success of these cars also fueled Chevrolet Division plans and revived factory participation in racing after more than two decades. This time, the factory openly pursued racing.

Several versions of the Lola chassis were built for Chevrolet engines and were raced by several teams. A total of twelve T-600 Lolas were eventually built, along with two T-610s built for Group C racing and four T-616s for smaller engines, for a grand total of eighteen in the T-600 line. The tenth car in the series became the first Corvette GTP, the non-race project car illustrated in the factory brochure and photography. The car that would have been the seventeenth in the T-600 series, and third in the T-610 line, received a number of suspension and detail updates and was designated variously as the T86/10, HU-8612/03, and T86/12 in Lola records. The chassis plate reads HU-8612/03. This was the fourth Hendrick Motorsports GM Goodwrench Corvette GTP and it raced only one time, in Columbus in '87, equipped with the Lotus active suspension.

The first and only T-710 built was loaned to General Motors and became the first GM Corvette GTP car to race. It was designed specifically for the turbocharged V6 engine and raced as the GM Goodwrench Corvette GTP. The T-711 was designed specifically for normally aspirated engines, and only one was built, although that car was designated by Lola as chassis number HU-711/02. That car was delivered in late 1984 to Lee Racing owner Lew Price of Pennsylvania.

## The Corvette GTP Legacy Begins

The Lee Racing car was fitted with a 6-liter, fuel-injected V8 and showed promise initially, but shakedown testing at Daytona proved to be a bigger shakedown than anticipated. The body did not fit well and continually broke mounting brackets, particularly on the rear body section that tended to move around on rough tracks. During testing a few weeks before the 24-Hours of Daytona, Price was coming off Turn 4 at upwards of 200 MPH when the rear wing mounts broke. The car lurched sideways, and the on-rushing wind blew the front and rear body panels off and ripped out the doors and windshield. Price brought the car to a stop with no more than the top body section in place. He had put only five or six laps on the car. Undeterred, the Lee Racing crew repaired the car, and co-drivers Carson Baird and Terry Labonte raced the Corvette GTP in the 24-Hours, though well down at the finish in fifty-first position and not running after 160 laps.

At Sebring, Baird and Labonte completed only twenty-seven laps and were not running at the flag. Baird raced the car at Charlotte, another DNF after fifty-three laps, and again at Mid-Ohio with another

*(opposite)* **In final form as shown, chassis number HU-8610/02's last race was Del Mar Fairgrounds (October 23, 1988) where Bobby Rahal qualified eleventh and finished fifth.**

DNF after twenty-three laps. Price and Chip Mead tried their hand at Watkins Glen but completed only fifty-nine laps. Then, at Watkins Glen 2, Price and Baird started sixteenth and finished eighth overall in a fifty-two car field, a welcome finish for a team struggling to overcome the car's blight of problems. In Round 16 at Columbus, Mead completed only seven laps, and Lee Racing rounded out the year at Daytona for the eighty-nine-lap Finale. Price, Baird, and Mead started fifteenth and finished tenth, a fine race for a completely independent team.

At about this time, a new project at Chevrolet emerged. It had been evolving for some time; the idea developed into a commitment to fund a single car and locate a team to race the car. Factory engineers saw that a racing car could be a test bed for several objectives. Instead of V8 power, they planned to use the car for development of a new generation engine, the turbocharged 90-degree V6 derived from production models, and new electronic management systems. In time, the GM Goodwrench Corvette GTP raced the small-block V8 as well, and both engines became forces to reckon with.

The car evolved from Brian Redman's original idea for GTP racing and became the most advanced Corvette of all time. The lifespan of a racing car is only a season or two—a result of continually changing competitive forces—and the Corvette GTP was to see its prime early on, though the cars were raced through 1988 as factory entries. The last Corvette GTP raced was HU-8810/01 fielded by Peerless Racing in 1988 and '89. Another chapter in road racing history ended when the Chevrolet-powered cars quietly rolled behind the wall of progress.

The Corvette GTP was designed for racing in America's most challenging series, the IMSA Camel GT, but thoughts continually drifted to the great French classic, the 24-Hours of Le Mans, and world championships. Le Mans remains the world's most prestigious and most celebrated race for sports cars. If the Corvette GTP could win that grueling enduro, it would be the crowning achievement in more than thirty years of racing with Chevrolet equipment and fill an empty spot in the division's legacy of road racing.

Ford had filled that empty spot with wins in 1966, '67, '68, '69, and '75. The 1975 victory was by Jackie Ickx and Derek Bell in the Gulf-Mirage powered by a 3-liter Ford-Cosworth V8. Bell would later prove an archadversary of the Corvette GTP as driver of Porsche 962s, and the Cosworth V8 saw IMSA duty as well, though it was never much of a threat.

After being fully developed in IMSA racing, the Corvette GTP had the potential of enhancing Chevrolet's international reputation by racing Le Mans and other International Group C events on the European calendar. Along with America's own IMSA GTP series, the new Lola-Chevy had quite a task ahead of it. As the IMSA cars developed, the European organizers added a class for the IMSA GTP cars to race alongside the International Group C cars, and IMSA cars became stars of Le Mans, although never overall winners.

Hurtle past the pits at Le Mans, then take the fast right-hander, roar under Dunlop Bridge, zigzag through the Esses and the right-hand Tertre Rouge leading onto the long Mulsanne Straight. This was the vision for Corvette GTP racing at Le Mans. Up through the gears to flat out on Mulsanne, perhaps 230 MPH for about five miles, then the sharp, 45 MPH right-hand Mulsanne Corner at the end, brake hard and downshift 5-4-3-2-1. Up through the gears again, and roar out of the turn followed by two or three dozen of the world's fastest cars in the hands of the most capable drivers ever assembled. Streak through left and right turns named Indianapolis and Arnage at the fastest speeds possible, through the Porsche turn, then Maison Blanche and the Ford kink, then back along the pit straight with exhaust wail reverberating off the walls and mixing with the roar of the massive crowd.

The car would have to endure more than 360 of these laps around the 8.47-mile circuit to win Le Mans. Lap after lap for twenty-four hours, day and night, rain or shine, for some seven thousand shifts around the Le Mans circuit; that was what the Corvette GTP would have to do to win the great event. Surviving this—the most famous endurance race of all time—places cars and drivers in a select and renowned league. Derek Bell was victorious

several times, as were Hurley Haywood, Klaus Ludwig, the Whittington brothers, Al Holbert, and several other drivers who campaigned in IMSA GTP.

While several factory engineers and planners discussed the possibilities, millions of Chevrolet enthusiasts around the world waited with great anticipation to see the Corvette GTP victorious, first in America and then Le Mans, then on to a World Manufacturers Championship. Ever since Ford captured its first World Sports Car Championship along with a World Grand Touring Prototype Championship in 1966, then repeated the World Sports Car title again in '67 followed by a World Championship for Makes in 1968, Chevrolet fans had carried an emptiness deep within them that the Corvette GTP was forecast to fill. It was, however, never to see the Le Mans circuit.

The original purpose of the Corvette GTP was twofold: to build Chevrolet competition prestige and to be an engineering test bed that would further develop Chevrolet's 90-degree V6 engine technology. That engine was little more than a shortened version of the small-block V8 and was extremely powerful in turbocharged form. If successful, it was likely to become a racing standard similar to the V8. Thus a market existed if the car could be as dominant as the T-600 and the March-Chevrolets proved to be with V8 power.

Comparing engine technologies with Ford, Chevrolet had no competitor for the legendary Ford-Cosworth DFV (Double Four Valve) engine that had dominated Grand Prix racing since its introduction in 1966. Its roots lay in Ford's 1964 Double Over Head Cam (DOHC) Indianapolis 500 engine that Jimmy Clark raced to victory in the Indy 500 of 1965. Later, the DOHC Ford dominated Indianapolis-style racing as a turbocharged engine, then became the Cosworth engine when Ford sought an outside builder.

While the Chevy Turbo-V6 in Grand Prix racing was low on the list of possibilities, Chevrolet stood to gain in both prestige and marketing with a winning small displacement racing engine. The Ilmor Indy V8 engine, which raced so successfully later at Indianapolis, followed the same development path as Ford's Cosworth and was actually designed and built by some of the same people who produced the Cosworth. Versions of the DFV, such as the larger

A

B

C

D

A. Early Corvette GTP development vehicle. Note the NACA ducts in the sides.

B. Ford's last win at Le Mans was the Jackie Ickx/Derek Bell victory in 1975 with the Cosworth-powered Gulf-Mirage finishing one-three overall.

C. Mario Andretti stands by while preparations are made for testing the Corvette GTP.

D. The Ford-Cosworth DFV proved its worth in endurance racing and as the winningest Formula One engine of all time, but in the Argo, it was an also-ran.

displacement endurance DFL engine, found their way into IMSA GTP racing with the Ford-Argo that Lyn St. James and other drivers raced in the mid-1980s. No record of the Ilmor in IMSA racing has been found.

With the resounding success of Redman's T-600, chassis manufacturers offered their cars with the capability of fitting a range of engines, and racing with Chevrolet power meant a larger market for Chevrolet. The small-block V8 had performed magnificently in the early 1980s, but GTP cars improved by 1985 and eclipsed the potential of the V8. The Turbo-V6 was a significant step up in performance, and the Corvette GTP was its showcase for Chevrolet. Its primary competitor was Porsche's turbocharged flat-six derived from the 911 line of production engines. Chevrolet's V8 had captured IMSA championships, displacing Porsche's dominance, but when the German cars returned with essentially the same engines as raced in the 935s but in new GTP and Group C cars, the Type 962 line, IMSA competition heated up. It was one thrilling showcase after another as American versus German engineering was showcased in cars handled by the best drivers in the world. Later, Japanese engineering would emerge as supreme in IMSA GTP racing.

Chevrolet Engineering specified the Corvette GTP body shape, and fabrication of the first T-710 was completed in the shops of Eric Broadley's famed Lola Cars, Ltd. in Huntington, England. Herb Fischel, manager of Chevrolet's High Performance Operations, described the process this way: "Our intent is to turn the knowledge gained through on-track experience into viable applications for our production cars and trucks. Thus, the rationale for the GTP Corvette: it's a rolling test bed for grooming our V6 to carry on the winning tradition of our small-block."

The major differences between the V8 T-600 and V6 T-710 were body shape and turbocharging, along with some chassis updates. Unlike the well-developed and normally aspirated 8-cylinder, the Turbo-V6 offered significant new ground for engineering. The Turbo-V6 was both smaller and lighter than the

**Porsche 935 Turbos won races as late as 1983. By the next year, March prototypes like this 84G of Dave Cowart and Kenper Miller with Chevrolet power emerged as the cars to beat.**

A&B. After Van Der Merwe set a track record pole and the fastest lap of the race, another track record, chassis HU-8610/ 01 burned at West Palm Beach (June 21, 1987). It was re-built with the original tub and raced five days later at Port-land, where Doc Bundy qualified fourth and finished seventh. Its last race was Del Mar Fairgrounds, October 25, 1987.

C. Chassis HU-8610/01.

D. HU-710/01 being rebuilt.

E. Chassis number HU-8610/02 was originally a long tail Turbo-V6 car converted over to a short tail V8 in May 1988.

F. Chassis HU-8610/02.

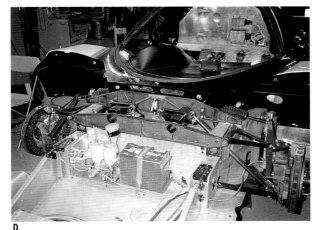

D

E

F

V8 and produced more horsepower, although with less torque at low RPM. Among many other advantages, the car's lower overall weight offered the benefit of reduced stress on components such as brakes, resulting in lighter parts and faster speeds through turns. The top speeds of both cars were similar, depending on gearing, but once in the power range, acceleration of the turbocharged Corvette GTP proved considerably quicker than the V8. However, low-speed exits from turns were better with the V8's quicker low-end torque and response.

The styling of the T-710 vaguely followed the lines of the 1985 Corvette to maintain some degree of product identification, although the wheelbase of the GTP was over ten inches longer, 106.5 inches compared to 96.2. The GTP was also about a foot longer overall, primarily because of its extended, aerodynamic nose that just cleared the ground by 2.5 inches. Its long tail also added to overall length. In the later short tail version, additional downforce was achieved with reduced weight overall.

The chassis of the car was aluminum sheet metal with a monocoque main section utilizing aircraft technology of riveted panels sandwiching lightweight honeycomb aluminum, a technique pioneered in racing cars by Ford in 1967. From pivot points located on the monocoque, the front suspension was composed of A-arms with coil-over shock absorbers. One interesting feature of the suspension's advanced pushrod and rocker arm design was its driver-operated capability. In the cockpit, a lever could be used to alter the angle of the suspension rocker blades so that the car's anti-roll capacity could be changed during a race. The rear suspension had a similar mechanism, also with driver control. With sixteen-inch diameter tires, 23.5 inches wide on the front and 27.0 on the rear, the Corvette GTP could exceed 2 G lateral acceleration, more than twice the production Corvette.

The aerodynamics of the racing cars were very different from those of production Corvettes. Because street cars are much heavier and are driven at far less demanding speeds, they must be good wind cheaters to maximize economy. The production line Corvette's drag coefficient of 0.341 provided a very slick design. The drag coefficient of a typical GTP car could be twice the value of a production car and would vary with wing and body positions. Racing aerodynamics added as much as four thousand pounds of downforce to a GTP car for very fast cornering while side-to-side stability in crosswinds was extremely high as well.

The body shape of the T-710 was actually an inverted wing or airfoil. The bottom of the car was flat, with an area of 32" x 40" as specified by IMSA and Group C regulations. The front and rear connections to the undertray were used to alter airflow. The low nose got under the air, forcing it over the car. The air that went under or through the car exited the rear through wide channels that funneled air upwards, where its velocity exceeded the velocity of the air moving over the top of the car, producing downforce. The wing added tremendously to this effect.

However, because downforce increases with air speed, the suspension must bear continually increasing loads as the car achieves flat-out speeds. The rear wing must supply a balance of load; too much will unnecessarily load the rear suspension, while maintaining the correct attitude to the air stream inhibits lift. Otherwise, the rear end of the car could become airborne as speed increases. Clearly, achieving the aerodynamic ideal for racing is a complex and demanding science. The car must be stable at all speeds and provide sufficient air movement through the car to sustain heat removal, particularly in turbocharged cars such as the Corvette GTP, and to provide ventilation for driver comfort. Extensive wind tunnel testing identified high drag, turbulent areas and contributed to designs for smoother airflow. Because of the high horsepower typical of GTP cars, insufficient downforce allowed tire spin that limited power to the ground and wasted tire mileage. The design of the GTP car took these requirements into account.

The Corvette GTP achieved minimum air resistance for high speeds and maximum downforce for proper adhesion, and did so with a stable platform. The Lola chassis also provided similar benefits to competitors. All four chassis in the T-810 series went to Nissan and were raced by Electramotive, only to be replaced by the cars of Japanese design and man-

A

A. Note the differences in ground effect treatments of rear sections.

B. Wind tunnel testing of the long tail configuration and single element wing, later to go to dual element and short tail.

C. The prototype Corvette GTP in the GM Wind Tunnel. Note the NACA duct air intake, soon changed to the much more open inlet, and the lack of an engine air inlet, yet to be developed.

D. Using the GM Wind Tunnel, the air inlet configuration was determined for the most even air flow distribution into the injectors of the V8 engine. The tufts of yarn show some of the airflow characteristics of the car.

E. Early Corvette GTP development vehicle. Chassis number HU 600/10 on loan to GM.

B

C

D

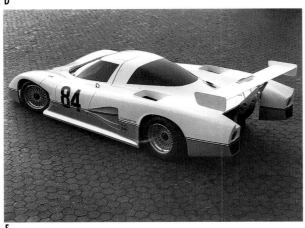

E

ufacture that rose to dominate the GTP series in the late 1980s. Corvette GTP cars raced with two body shapes and three chassis designations. The bodies were the long tail and short tail. Chassis designation began with the loaned T-710/01, then all three updated cars in the T-8610 line, the single T-8710 Lola built, and the single T-8810 built. The Hendrick Motorsports team raced all five of the chassis supplied with General Motors connections. The last car built was the Peerless Racing Corvette GTP.

The long tail was initially thought to produce greater downforce but did so with a longer car that had the disadvantage of greater weight than the short tail car. The shorter version eventually proved to be as effective as the long tail version. In either case, the GTP shape and large wing kept the car glued to the ground in turns, yet allowed extremely high speeds of greater than 210 MPH.

Engine compartment air inlets on the sides of the body were initially a National Advisory Committee for Aeronautics (NACA) concept to introduce cooling air with the least disturbance of the air's slipstream. Incoming air went through large radiators required to keep engine temperatures in the desired operating range. The right side radiator cooled the engine and transaxle. The left side radiator cooled the turbocharger intercooler. Body openings were minimized but included two snorkels atop the rear suspension towers to direct cooling air toward the rear brakes. The front of the body, similar to the production Corvette shape, enclosed two inlets for air cooling of front brakes.

The GTP body was made of high strength Kevlar fabric bonded with epoxy resin. The reason for using Kevlar was its high strength in thin sections and its ability to retain its strength when exposed to elevated temperatures, such as those generated by turbocharging. Engine compartment temperatures can exceed 300°F and damage less heat-resistant materials.

The stark interior was fitted with only the essentials for driver control and system instrumentation. Other than a second seat required by Group C regulations, the driver had the barest necessities for enduring hours of high G forces, gearshifts, and steering wheel feedback. In a semi-reclining position

facing a small diameter steering wheel, 1.75 turns lock-to-lock, all controls and engine monitors were within arm's reach for racing on the very edge of physics. Provisions were made for the driver to alter front/rear brake balance from the cockpit, along with turbo boost control and anti-roll alterations.

Overall, the Corvette GTP was an impressive showcase for Chevrolet engineering. The car's heavy-duty cast iron V6 block was adapted from a variety of production GM cars, although displacement was reduced to 209 cubic inches from the standard 229. Stroke was reduced from 3.48 inches to 2.75, and bore was increased to 4.0 inches from 3.74 to produce a more favorable over-square form. The block was a Chevrolet Special Products Bow Tie release. The 1985 and '86 blocks varied slightly; the latter was redesigned for a one-piece rear main seal rather than two-piece, and parts were not interchangeable. Heavy duty internals and cast aluminum heads were over-the-counter Chevrolet off-road production items from the factory's extensive performance parts catalog.

The heads were closed chamber with 64 cc volume that delivered a modest compression ratio of 7.5:1. Rather than using sophisticated overhead cams and exotic materials characteristic of the Porsche 962, the Chevrolet engine was a conventional overhead valve design with a single internal cam that actuated 2.05-inch diameter intake and 1.6-inch exhaust valves similar to a vast number of high performance Chevrolet engines raced over the years.

Using a compact Warner-Ishi Model RX9-L turbocharger, maximum boost of 20 PSI, produced 775 HP from the Turbo-V6 as first raced. Later, engine wizard Ryan Falconer pushed output up to around 900 HP and eventually exceeded 1,100 HP, according to some sources. Such a powerful engine was most often used for qualifying and setting record laps but was not sufficiently durable for racing to win. The turbo was mounted aft of the engine to benefit from external cooling airflow ducted into the engine compartment. The turbo intercooler reduced combustion chamber inlet air temperature to around 100°F from about 300°F. High pressure multi-port fuel injection fed combustion chambers, but because of the

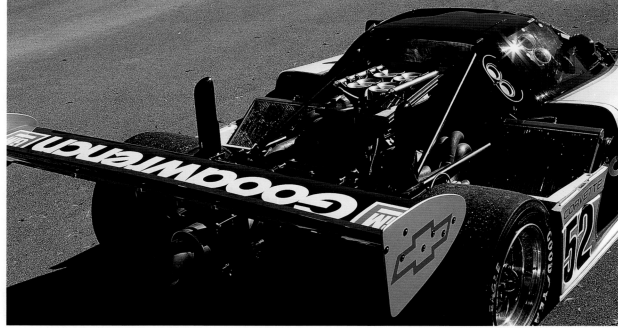

Chassis number HU-8610/02, final configuration.

A

A. Testing at Laguna Seca with Broadley, Mario Andretti (in driver's suit), and Tony Cicale, October 1984.

B. Smokey wants to drive, but there's no helmet for him! Starting sixth, engine failure sidelined the car after 151 laps at Sebring.

B

to handle the Corvette GTP project. Initially I didn't get directly involved with engine development; that was Bill Howell, a Chevrolet engineer with deep racing connections all the way back to the early Trans-Am days. He worked closely with Ryan Falconer and other engine builders around the country.

The way our group worked, we had a person for engines, a separate person for the vehicle, another for the chassis, and so on. We didn't have a person for electronics. In fact, we didn't even have a program manager; each of us simply had a project that we were responsible for. All the conceptual development was around the Turbo-V6 because we thought IMSA was the best place to show off the engine's potential. The rules lent themselves to that size engine, so it was a natural fit. Again, the car we came up with was a show car, not a race car by any means. It was never intended to be raced. Although we did race programs primarily, we also did show cars, pace cars, magazine concept cars, a lot of things around the country to promote our products, including hard core race programs.

There seemed to be continued interest from our management to get into competition with that car, so we commissioned Lola Cars to build a proper racing car around that engine package. That was during the winter of 1983. The very first track exposure for the car was in England in the spring of 1984 during tests conducted by Lola Cars at Goodwood. The driver was Jonathan Palmer, a Formula One driver, who Lola hired for the day. That was the debut of the car.

There was no team based in the U.S. to pick up the program and keep it running when we brought the car to Warren. We had a car, but without a team and a driver, without an organization over here, nothing actually happened with it. The car sat around through the entire year of 1984. We did a little testing with it in California, but there was no team, no driver, no organization, and no sponsor to fund the program. It was questionable at that point that the program would continue.

Our management saw some marketing potential, and GM Goodwrench saw some opportunities as well. Word had gotten around that we had a car, and the Rick Hendrick people expressed interest,

although they had no experience in road racing. I don't know who approached who first, but since everyone knew each other, it probably grew out of mutual discussions about racing. I think that Rick viewed the program as a challenge, a new adventure for them and fun stuff to do.

The intent of the program from Chevrolet's side of it was always to win races, but being realistic, we had to accept the fact that we were new at GTP racing, we were developing an engine, a car, new electronics, and a new team all at once. There was little hope of winning the first few races, but we always set our sights to win. Our goals were not simply just to be there—to go out to give exposure to the product, the sponsor, and the driver. On the other hand, we had to be honest and tell ourselves that we would have growing pains for a while, and we did—many of them.

One of the goals was to show people in the racing community the capability of the V6. They had not gotten excited about the potential of the engine to race with the best in the world. There were a few limitations on the engine, such as the amount of boost into the engine. Porsche was very successful with the turbocharged 6-cylinder engine, and we thought the best way to beat them was to build a better engine. Ford was there; Buick had a parallel program in GM; it was a horsepower war. At times, the engines were in the 900-plus horsepower range. It didn't make any sense. Engine development was out of control, in any real sense.

At the time, that much horsepower was seen as a good thing, but upon reassessment, the reliability was not that good. If you look at racing, a high percentage of cars that drop out do so because of mechanical problems. That much horsepower just overstresses the entire car, the brakes, the transmission, the cooling system. IMSA then started putting restrictions on the amount of boost that could be run, and that brought racing back under control. The tracks that the cars raced on didn't need 1,000 horsepower, like Lime Rock, or Road Atlanta. Or even Watkins Glen, where the cars were going two hundred miles per hour. That really didn't make a lot of sense, but escalation got into it; the other guy was

doing this, doing that, so to keep up you had to do what they were doing and a little bit more.

There was no primary target, such as beating Ford. There were a lot of cars out there. Porsche had the reliability and experience, and there were a lot of them out there, 935s and 962s. Buick was there, BMW, Jaguar, all of them were competitors that made a lot of good racing, and exciting racing with all the factory involvement. From the reliability standpoint, Porsche was the primary target. There were so many of them, they were the benchmark in the beginning of the program, then Nissan came in and proved to be strong. The racing drew good crowds, but it was very, very expensive.

The Corvette and GM Goodwrench people saw the name exposure very favorably. The Goodwrench people did a lot of promotions with their parts and service networks around the country and with their Mr. Goodwrench advertising. They capitalized on the racing quite a bit by bringing their people to the tracks to show them an exciting weekend of racing. Most of the promotional programs were funded by GM Goodwrench.

GM Goodwrench was also heavily involved with NASCAR racing at the time, so the Corvette nameplate, among other GM nameplates, wasn't of particular interest in the GTP program. From Chevrolet's perspective, Corvette and Camaro are viewed as the performance nameplates, and Corvette as the flagship of the Chevrolet line. It has a worldwide reputation and is viewed as world class. Other divisions of GM like to use the Corvette nameplate because it is a corporate nameplate that everyone in the world recognizes. So, although the GTP car could have been called something else among GM nameplates, Corvette provided the greatest performance recognition.

The first win, at Road Atlanta, was a really exciting day, but the program had been quite a struggle, and finally we got a victory. Then, just a couple of months later, we won again at West Palm Beach. Those wins in 1986 were the high-water marks of the entire program and proved the performance potential of the concept. There had been a lot of bumps in the road getting there; we had been devel-

oping an engine, and it proved to be a winner. We had fairly small crews, both the race crew and here at Chevrolet. With only about three people working on the program, it was an ambitious undertaking to attempt to do all the things that racing required, plus development of an electronic management system. Eventually, the competition caught up with us. The Nissan people came on the scene with a big operation in California that raised the level of investment required to be competitive, from the sheer numbers of people. Unfortunately, our program tended to fade after 1986.

Primary among our objectives was to win a long-distance race, either Sebring or Daytona, because those races were known as endurance races, and that was what we were trying to prove with our program. We would have made a bigger impression on everyone if we had won at Daytona where we sat on the pole. So, not winning either Sebring or Daytona was a disappointment, certainly. Other failures along the way were just part of racing, but overall, we did fairly well.

One limitation was that we didn't have control of the car design, it being done by Lola, so we didn't have the input we should have had. In hindsight, we should have done things in that regard a little differently. Our drivers were very good and made up for deficiencies the car itself displayed. Anyone who had gone to an IMSA race and seen Sarel knew he could drive. He was pretty spectacular—very, very quick. With Ken Howes as team manager, we were introduced to Sarel by Ken. They had won the Daytona 24-Hours a few years earlier in the Kreepy Krauly Porsche. Everybody knew Doc Bundy, who had some success with the GTP Jaguar team. He was available, and we had seen him and thought he would be a good partner with Sarel. That match worked out pretty well. Doc was actually at the wheel of both victories, Road Atlanta and West Palm Beach.

After our big year in 1986, IMSA changed the rules with further restrictions on turbo engines. They had a sliding scale of weight-to-displacement, and it appeared that they were giving some advantages to the V8. It was a simpler package. We didn't have to

worry about turbochargers and intercoolers, waste gates and things of that type. We thought that for simplicity and the weight advantage, it would be desirable to go to the V8 to replace the V6. Well, I guess we underestimated the potential of the Turbo-V6 because Nissan rose to dominate the GTP series during those years, and then Toyota came along and picked up where they left off. The V8 was reliable, but it wasn't quick enough, and not as successful as we had hoped. We thought that the V8 was such a tried and true package that we could put an aluminum V8 in the car and it would be trouble free. That was essentially true, but it just wasn't quick enough.

The Corvette GTP program spanned about ten years. We went through the evolution of the Turbo-V6, then we had the V8. In the later years, we had a variety of fuel systems and management systems and we worked on a lot of technical details. For the big picture, for what we were trying to accomplish, we had some measurable and noteworthy successes, and developed a lot of hardware and knowledge that is compiled in GM high performance parts and equipment catalogs. I think we offer the broadest cross section of high performance parts available anywhere for whatever venue. We've shown over the years that the selection of Bow Tie parts available, whether V6, V8, small-block, or big-block, are affordable and they get the job done, whether boat racing or GTP racing.

From a personal standpoint, GTP racing was really exciting. The cars were very fast, made a lot of noise, and gave spectators some of the best sports car racing ever seen in this country. For me to be part of it with the Corvette GTP was quite exciting. ➤

**(opposite) Winning at Road Atlanta! Van Der Merwe set the pole with a track record and set the fastest lap of the race with another track record. Teamed with Doc Bundy, they set a race average speed record with overall victory; from pole to victory lane, a clean sweep for the Corvette GTP.**

# The Competition

The March-Chevrolets, GTP Jaguars, and the growing number of Porsche 962s fought it out in the early races of 1985 with the 962 winning all but one race that year—that one going to the XJR-5 Jag of Brian Redman and Hurley Haywood at Road Atlanta. Al Holbert won the IMSA Championship with nine wins in the Löwenbräu Special Porsche. During that year, a new GTP car emerged. The Lola chassis Nissan GTP, the T-810 line, handled by Don Devendorf and Tony Adamowicz, showed potential early on, a portent of things to come in GTP racing. Later, the Nissan team raced its own chassis and dominated the series four years running.

The first showing of the Goodwrench Corvette GTP was at Road America on August 25, 1985, for the Löwenbräu Classic, won by Drake Olsen and Derek Bell in the Dyson Racing Budweiser Porsche 962. Klaus Ludwig, teaming with Doc Bundy, was the fastest qualifier with a new record of 1:59.88 in the rear engine Mustang Probe GTP, the official Ford Motor Company entry, while Bell set the fastest race lap at 2:02.66, also a new record. David Hobbs and Sarel Van Der Merwe started eleventh in the GM Goodwrench Corvette GTP and completed only sixty-nine laps to wind up not running at the finish, ending up in thirty-third place in a field of fifty-five cars.

The Hendrick team missed the following race at Pocono, then Hobbs and Vern Schuppan qualified promisingly high at seventh on the grid at Watkins Glen for the New York 500. Ludwig again set the fastest race lap in the Mustang Probe GTP, but was out in thirty-eight laps. Unfortunately, the Goodwrench Corvette GTP went out just nine laps later and finished well down from the tenth overall of the Lew Price/Carson Baird Lee Racing Corvette GTP that carried the day for Chevrolet.

At Columbus, Ludwig was again fastest in the Mustang Probe GTP shared with Bundy, and Hobbs qualified the Goodwrench GTP car sixth, but by the sixteenth lap, both the Goodwrench and Lee Racing entries were out. The Ludwig/Bundy Ford GTP was out by lap fifty-seven, and Porsche won again.

In the final round of the season, the Daytona Finale, Van Der Merwe showed the potential of the Goodwrench Corvette GTP by streaking to a record qualifying lap at 1:38.88 (129.61 MPH), and team driver Bill Adam set the fastest race lap at 1:41.55, also a new record. Unfortunately, the car lasted just sixty-five laps, and the team earned $250 for its efforts. However, this end-of-season surge indicated that the car had enormous potential, and visions of dominating the 1986 IMSA GTP season became the talk among Chevrolet fans.

By the end of the '85 season, it was clear that GTP was the domain of the professionals. Sponsorships had steadily increased, as had the cost of racing. Along with the factories supporting top teams, tire manufacturers made every race of the series a heated contest in which the winning tires quickly became advertisements for winning cars.

*(opposite)* **IMSA GTP competition was fierce in 1986, making it a thrilling racing series followed by millions of fans. Here, the March-Chevrolet of Al and Art Leon leads eventual winner, the Dyson Racing Porsche, and the Bob Akin Racing Porsche. The Porsches were tough in 1986.**

B

A

C

Goodyear, Bridgestone, Yokohama, BFGoodrich, and independents on Hoosiers pushed GTP racing into a tire war.

Later Dunlop joined the fray. Fallout from this high buck involvement was a steady stream of rumor and intrigue about new and better tire compounds, which teams had what sponsorships, who would be running what tire, which drivers would be driving for what team, which teams really had the level of support required to be competitive, what rule changes were expected and how the cars would be affected, and endless political maneuvering that brought incessant backstage jockeying by teams trying to gain any advantage in both hardware and financing, neither of which ever seemed to be enough.

Because the Porsches had shown so well, Bob Tullius campaigned to get new weight requirements for the Porsche 962s, and 130 pounds were added for the '86 season. In addition to more weight, all turbo cars started the new season with another penalty. Driver-adjustable turbo boost had been debated throughout the '85 season. It was an advantage that normally aspirated engines did not possess, but turning up the boost used more fuel, so the Porsche camp argued that the advantage went to non-turbo cars that required fewer pit stops for fuel. While Porsche teams kept mum about the real potential of their cars, the debate simmered, then came to a boil when Hans Stuck knocked almost seven seconds off the Sebring lap record in Bob Akin's Coca-Cola sponsored 962. The 962s were sandbagging all along.

Then there were Van Der Merwe and Adam setting blinding qualifying and lap records in the final race of the season at Daytona. The turbo cars had a great power advantage at Daytona, even though "limited" to a single turbo and single ignition. The shaping of the rules raged on, and the rule makers were faced with a dilemma: if Porsche continued to dominate, the Ford, Chevrolet, Jaguar, Nissan, BMW, and independent teams might throw up their hands in disgust and quit, and the GTP series would die the same death that ended the Can-Am, a thrilling series killed by Porsche domination in the early '70s.

Tullius and other stock block based teams got the rule change they had asked for; the "turn up the boost" knob was eliminated from all cars. Suddenly, the 6-liter V12 Jags and V8-powered cars were in a more favorable position, but how much more could not be determined until well into the next season. By the last race, Tullius's Group 44 Jags had won only two races while the Porsches took thirteen and the championship again. V8-powered cars won none. To survive, IMSA needed all the best cars and drivers, but rather than simply survive, GTP racing blossomed as one of the world's finest series, and was so hotly contested that fans poured into racetracks everywhere and TV broadcasts took the events to the world.

The 1986 GTP season was a wonder to behold. Outwardly, the cars were seen as essentially unlimited racing cars, free of the fuel rules that stymied much of European racing. At the start of the IMSA season, Porsche's dominance came under severe doubt. A wide variety of manufacturers entered well-proven cars, and many world class drivers and well-experienced teams with highly competitive cars had the potential of winning anywhere. As the year progressed from race to race, the manufacturers continued to enter their cars in what became an exciting—if not the most exciting—season of GTP racing.

While the Group 44 Jaguar team was the only front-runner without turbocharging, the Bob Tullius cars had speed, durability, and better fuel economy than the turbo cars. Chevrolet entered the season with the Goodwrench Corvette GTP in full form. But there was John Paul, Jr. in a quick Turbo-V6 March-Buick, and the Lee Racing Corvette GTP was back for the first three races. Then there was the Zakspeed Ford team with German champion driver Ludwig in the 2.1-liter Turbo-4 Mustang Probe. But apparently he did not perform to Ford Dearborn's satisfaction because a split occurred mid-season and Ford went with Roush Racing to run the factory GTP Ford powered by a small displacement turbo Cosworth V8. Zakspeed chose to stay with its inline Turbo-4.

BMW moved into the GTP class with two superb, 800 HP turbo 2-liter, 4-cylinder March chassis cars

**A. Turbo cars of all types belched flames on down shifting. Van Der Merwe enters Charlotte's tricky Carousel, Turn 2.**

**B. A.J. Foyt and Bob Wollek won the 12-Hours of Sebring in this Porsche 962.**

**C. Arch-competitor to Goodyear, BFGoodrich, and Bridgestone, Bob Akin Racing ran Yokohama tires. Akin teamed with Hans Stuck (German) and Jo Gartner (Austrian) to win Sebring, setting race distance and speed records, and winning by eight laps ahead of the Busby/BFGoodrich 962. Sadly, Gartner was killed at Le Mans that year.**

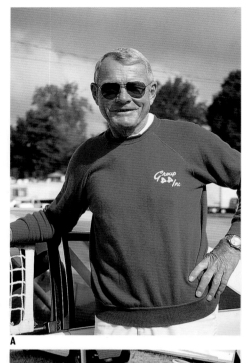

A

B

C

D

E

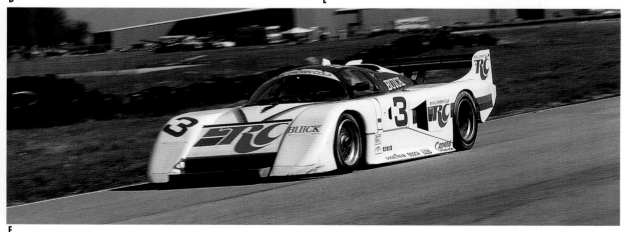

F

entered by McLaren North America. Although the cars showed well in the hands of top drivers, BMW withdrew from GTP after the '86 season.

The Devendorf Lola-Nissan GTP entries were close on everyone's heels and moving up. They did not quit, and Porsche drivers soon found themselves chasing the Nissans.

Although Porsche won twelve races that year, six by Holbert—a repeat championship—Chevrolet, Ford, BMW, and Jaguar won at least one race each. Surprisingly, the Camel Light cars, supposedly the equals of the GTP cars in terms of power-to-weight ratio, were often eclipsed by the GTO cars, particularly the Jack Roush Mustangs that began the season with a fourth and fifth overall at Daytona behind the winning Porsche 962 entries.

For the first time, all seventeen of the IMSA races were televised, so millions more fans watched the races at home. Rule changes that year centered around additional weight required for the turbo cars in an attempt to restrain them somewhat and to improve the prospects of normally aspirated cars. What the fans got was exceptional racing by an exceptional lineup of the world's top drivers: Sarel Van Der Merwe, Doc Bundy, Geoff Brabham, David Hobbs, Al Holbert, Klaus Ludwig, Derek Bell, Al Unser, Jr., Hans Stuck, A.J. Foyt, Danny Sullivan, Arie Luyendyk, Davy Jones, Bob Tullius, Chip Robinson, Bob Akin, Jan Lammers, Brian Redman, Hurley Haywood, John Watson, Bob Wollek, Bobby Rahal, and dozens more who turned in outstanding drives, making IMSA racing fiercely competitive that year. This was the field that the Goodwrench Corvette GTP team faced for 1986.

That year proved to be enormously competitive in IMSA. Van der Merwe began where he left off at Daytona the year before by setting the fastest qualifying lap at 1:39.32, one-half second off the record he set three months earlier. Teaming with Doc Bundy, he set the pole for the twenty-four hour race, but problems began early, and the car did not start. The Lee Racing entry was the only Corvette GTP in the race, but it lasted only 107 laps.

At Miami, frustrations piled up when both the Hendrick and Lee Racing Corvette GTP entries were out after thirty laps. At Sebring, only the Lee Racing 'Vette was entered, again an early departure. Porsche claimed wins in both races with one-two-three sweeps. The Goodwrench team prepped their entry for Road Atlanta, the home track for co-driver Doc Bundy. Van der Merwe set the fastest lap with a blistering absolute track record of 1:12.001, a full second quicker than the highest qualifying Porsche, the Holbert Racing 962.

After setting the pace for a few laps, the intake temperature inched up, and Van Der Merwe backed off to run third a few seconds behind the leaders, John Paul, Jr. in the Conte Racing Buick Hawk running behind Holbert's Porsche. The pace slowed somewhat, and on lap thirty-four a spun car under the bridge at Turn 11 prompted some quick thinking by Van Der Merwe. The Goodwrench 'Vette led the dash into the pits just as the caution came out and assured a leading position behind the pace car. Bundy took over, and with the fuel topped off, he was second behind Holbert who pitted on lap forty-five. The Corvette GTP surged into the lead until the next pit on lap sixty-eight when Holbert regained the lead. Van der Merwe took over, but somehow got his cool suit hose lodged under the shoulder harness and had to drive with it unbuckled. He held on against the G forces, managing to set the race's fastest overall lap at 1:14.41 on lap eighty-three. John Paul, Jr. was hot on the Corvette's tail when the team's last pit stop took place on lap 104. Bundy took over and held off Paul, making it a tight race until the Buick pitted for fuel. That left the win to Bundy, who sailed to victory with a twenty-nine second margin in the 124-lap race.

Suddenly, the Corvette GTP had speed, quickness, durability, and a victory. Just as Redman had done with the Chevrolet-powered Cooke-Woods Lola, the Porsche string was broken at sixteen straight wins with the Lola-Chevy GTP victory. The jubilant crowd saw history made, the first-ever IMSA Grand Touring Prototype win by Chevrolet. The Hendrick Motorsports GTP team had its act together, and forecasts of dominating the series quickly spread among enthusiastic fans. Little did they know that the heat of competition had just turned up a notch,

**A.** Bob Tullius fielded one of the top professional teams in IMSA GTP racing. An excellent driver himself, with many wins to his credit, he was both team owner and driver.

**B.** The Group AA 6.0-liter Jaguar XJR-7 engine was the "big cat" for 1986. At 650 HP, it was at a 150 horsepower disadvantage to the BMW Turbo-4 (800 HP) and perhaps 500 HP to the Ryan Falconer built Turbo-V6 GM Goodwrench Corvette GTP.

**C.** The Argo JM16 chassis fitted with production-based Buick engine shows the diversity of chassis/engine combinations that heated up GTP racing in 1984. In 1985, these cars were classified as Camel Lights.

**D.** Sebring's 12-Hours enduro means night racing. The Hendrick Motorsports crew during night practice.

**E.** Al Holbert dominated GTP racing in 1986. In sixteen starts he won six races with two seconds and two thirds. Porsche was king.

**F.** IMSA GTP veteran John Paul, Jr. fielded this Buick-powered March 84G.

*(below)* The Buick Hawk (March) of Whitney Ganz and Bob Lobenberg performed excellently at Charlotte, finishing third overall, just one lap back from the winners in the 500 km Camel GT race, showing that GM stock block engines were competitive.

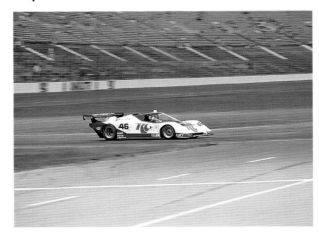

A

B

*(opposite)* Practice at Mid-Ohio (May 1987). Sarel Van Der Merwe and Doc Bundy qualified fifth and finished third in the Champion Spark Plug 500 km.

A. Al Holbert and Derek Bell were described as racing's best team. Holbert won both the 24-Hours of Daytona and Le Mans in 1986, and was IMSA champion for the fifth time.

B. IMSA GTP racing was spelled Nissan ZX-Turbo from 1988 through '91.

A

B

A. Ford's factory entry, the Mustang Probe, showed flashes of brilliance with Klaus Ludwig, who set the pole and won at Laguna Seca. It was the most advanced car in GTP racing.

B. The BFGoodrich Porsches raced on their sponsor's tires, street type radials, at a time when a tire war raged in racing. This car had a commanding lead until hitting debris on the track. Damaged, the car dropped to twenty-sixth.

literally, because a new Lola (8610/01) for the Hendrick team was expected in May, and it had better cooling to allow increased turbo boost. Engine man Ryan Falconer was turning up Chevrolet power, and a two-car Goodwrench team was to be fielded in sprint races.

The Turbo-V6 Chevy won the pole position, set a new track record while qualifying (124.998 MPH), and went on to win the 310-mile race at Road Atlanta by establishing a new race average speed record of 120.951 MPH. The Corvette GTP's first victory, April 6, 1986, was by the first of the Hendrick Lola cars, T-710/01. With the power-laden Corvette GTP's first win taken in convincing fashion, fans and competitors alike began looking more closely at the fastest Corvette and remembered the screaming yellow Cooke-Woods Lola, but it would be several more races before a Chevrolet found the winner's circle again.

The GTP Corvette's second and last win occurred in the tenth round of the season, the three-hour Grand Prix of West Palm Beach, Florida, in its inaugural running on June 6, 1986—another Corvette GTP pole and victory and a sweltering day. Both Road Atlanta and West Palm Beach were in the string of seven poles set by Van Der Merwe that established a new IMSA record. At West Palm Beach, rain delayed everything and sand found its way onto the track, making the course so tricky that several cars crashed in testing. The track was little more than 1.6 miles of drag races through city streets connected by hairpin turns that favored the V12 Jaguars rather than turbocharged cars.

The victory at West Palm Beach came down to the last turn, the final drag race, and a three-car mix-up. Redman, leading into the turn in a Jag, was driving with a broken radio and was unaware that it was the final turn. Bundy went deep into the turn close behind and was pushed into Redman by the third car. The nudging spun Bundy into the correct line for the final sprint, and he stood on it to win by just under four tenths of a second.

Brian Redman recalls that finish:

"Yes, the race with Doc at West Palm Beach was most interesting. We had various problems through the race, but our Jaguar was the fastest car in the field. From having been two laps down at one time, we had got back onto the lead lap through the great good fortune, on two occasions, of having just overtaken the leading car in the race when there was a full course yellow with the pace car. This meant that each time the pace car picked up the leader, and because we had just overtaken the leader (although the first time, two laps down and the second time, one lap down), we were able to gain a lap back.

"Danny Ongais had crashed towards the end of the race. The pace car came out and we followed it round, the order being Bundy, a BFGoodrich 962, Derek Bell (who was a lap down, but driving like his life depended on it), and myself. When the green flag waved, I knew there would be a lot of confusion, so I hung back a little going into Turn 1. There was a lot of pushing and shoving going on, and both Derek and I passed the BFGoodrich 962. The next to the last corner, Derek hit Doc, and I passed both of them. However, the final corner was a very tight left-hander that I hadn't enough lock to get round without pulling over to the right to gain room. As soon as I moved right, I knew it was a mistake because Doc pulled inside me, and I couldn't turn. To cap it all, so did the BFG Porsche! It might have helped if I'd known it was the last lap (the radio was broken), as I would have stayed left and brought the car through by sliding the back round. However, hindsight is 20/20!

"The GTP years were, by and large, good years. But as always happens, the team with the greatest technological resources (i.e., money) usually comes through to win, and effectively destroys the opposition, which then drops out, leaving weak fields."

Van Der Merwe's driving shone brilliantly in consistent high speed blasts on every track and provided great excitement and anticipation for Chevrolet fans who were certain that the string of poles could be turned into a string of victories. The GM Goodwrench cars did not win as often as they set poles and records for many reasons, such as mechanical or electrical failures, but most losses were due to the fact that these cars were development vehicles for factory engineers who used racing as a test bed.

Racing teams painstakingly refine their cars to win, and testing new ideas at the races is considered a sure formula for failure. Even so, Hendrick Motorsports fielded an excellent GTP team with proven potential. They had the capability of consistent wins along with Bundy's superb driving that took the checkered flag for both victories. Even though the final tally for that year—two wins and several near misses—was an excellent showing, it was disappointing to see the Porsches dominate race after race when the Corvette prototypes dropped out early.

During the later races of the '86 season, Van Der Merwe was particularly impressed with the car and commented that, "When the car is set up properly and the engine running at full power, the Hendrick Corvette is *the* force to reckon with." Two Goodwrench Corvettes were entered at Daytona for the final event, and Wally Dallenbach, Jr. joined the team. Then, broken exhaust pipe bolts sidelined both cars as Bob Tullius and Chip Robinson took the Finale in their Group 44 Jag.

However, the 1986 GTP season was so fiercely fought that drivers the caliber of Brian Redman, A.J. Foyt, John Watson, David Hobbs, John Paul, Jr., Geoff Brabham, Danny Sullivan, and many other top international drivers came up empty in the win column. It was, indeed, a season to behold. And Chevrolet had given it a decidedly American flavor in what was described as a development year, a tune-up for the following season. With Chevrolet's motorsports team led by Herb Fischel and GM Goodwrench sponsorship handled by Sam McAllister, and with Corvette GTP team manager John Pierce and factory engine man Richard Johnson, along with Ryan Falconer and an excellent team, the Hendrick Motorsports team had become a frontline competitor in world class racing, and sights were set to win the 1987 IMSA Camel GT championship.

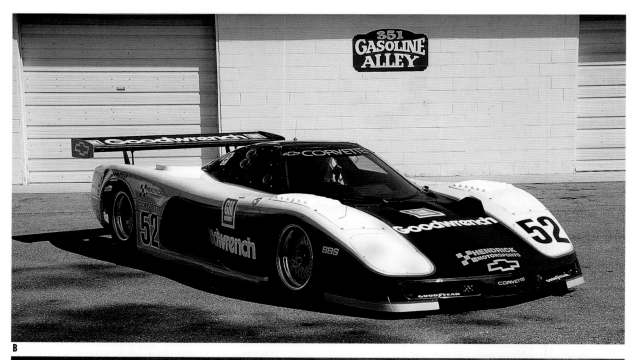

B

A

C

finish with a win. That was the last official race under Chevrolet sponsorship.

We started running the Corvette GTP in long tail form with the V6. We got into the short tail form when we went to the V8. By then, there was a lot of chassis development going on, and the short tail form was really the result of wind tunnel testing. It came about because the chassis wasn't as competitive as we needed it to be. It was like a desperate effort to try and keep up with the Jags. I maintain that, if at any point in time had General Motors decided to go with an updated chassis, be it '87 or '88, even '89, the power was available to make the car a winner, be it V6 or V8. I really think that our problems centered around the chassis, not the engine in either form. I think either engine would have won races.

On paper the car was a winner. But in practice, we had a lot of problems with the fuel management system in the car, for starters, and General Motors was, at that time, hell-bent on developing their own system. The Bosch system was available, and we could have bought it. I think a lot of time and effort, and money, was spent on development of the General Motors system. I would not have minded carrying on development of the General Motors system, had they carried on racing with the Bosch system. I think, in terms of fuel consumption, that the General Motors system was quite disastrous. At that point in time, had we gone with the Bosch system and won races, while testing with the GM system, it could have worked out much better. The basic package of the car, especially in '86, was so good that it could have taken on anybody in the world.

The greatest success we had with the car was the first time we won, that was at Road Atlanta. The biggest disappointment is that I think that car could have won ten times more if we had not been hampered with corporate decisions. At that time, I was racing Porsches in Europe, including the factory team, and I knew how good the Corvette GTP package really was. I think that car could have won at least another ten races, if we had not been hampered by corporate decisions,

"save your ass" kinds of decisions. That's probably the saddest thing about the car; it was absolutely a super car.

I had no problem, personally, with the factory people. It was my first exposure to "Corporate America," and I think that the guys working on the car knew what they wanted to do, but they did not have the ultimate authority to do what they wanted to do. I think the project was screwed up at the corporate level because it was the car that could have done everything everyone expected of it. At the end, it got killed in the red tape.

The Hendrick team was the hub of everything; all the feedback to the factory came from the team. Everything they did came from us. We did the testing and told them of our findings, especially in the early days of the management system, which was all going wrong. Ryan Falconer, the engine builder at the time, was very involved as well. So, all the feedback to the factory came from the Hendrick team.

It's really quite sad that this car was never brought to its full potential, but I will always be grateful that I had the opportunity of driving one of the most exciting cars ever built. I think the Corvette GTP will rate with the pre-war Mercedes and Auto-Union Grand Prix cars—certainly at that level. ➤

**A. The Tom Walkinshaw Racing Jaguars entered IMSA racing in 1987 and changed the equation, winning the Daytona 24-Hours in 1988.**

**B&C. Chassis HU-8610/01.**

# Team Corvette

uilding on 1986 successes and with IMSA's fastest driver, the following year was predicted to be the year of the Hendrick Motorsports Corvette GTP. Plans were laid to run the entire sixteen-race schedule, including endurance races at Daytona and Sebring. Once again, IMSA rule changes favored stock block cars, and some of the advantages of the Chevrolet Turbo-V6 were taken away.

Turbos were limited to one, and displacement of two-valve per cylinder engines was reduced to three liters. Overall weight of four-valve per cylinder turbocharged cars was increased. All GTP cars raced with a minimum weight of 2,050 pounds, and all the turbo cars were considered to be on the same footing for the first time. Once again, normally aspirated cars were favored, however the 650 HP Jaguar V12 at 5.3 liters was well off the potential of the 800-plus HP turbocharged cars. Although the Jags were more fuel efficient, requiring one less fuel stop in a three hundred mile race, Tullius's Group 44 Jags won only one race in '86.

Tullius returned for the '87 season with XJR-7 and later with new XJR-8 cars and continued to maintain that no equitable formula existed for normally aspirated cars racing against turbocharged cars. His Jaguars were considered to have win potential only in long distance races, while the turbo cars were predicted to contest the championship that would be won on sprint courses. IMSA also imposed a two-percent rule that allowed cars with stock block push-rod engines to run with two percent less weight, thus favoring the Chevrolet- and Buick-powered cars over the Porsches and Jaguars.

Meanwhile, BMW North America withdrew from the Camel GT. Davy Jones had crashed one of the BMW GTP cars at Road America, involving Van Der Merwe in a Hendrick Corvette (8610/01), and Porsche domination was too much to contend with. Coca-Cola, longtime sponsor of Bob Akin Racing, also withdrew. The Nissan GTP team announced it would run a limited schedule, as did Tullius, who dropped out of nine of the sixteen events. Interest in the IMSA GTP also waned at Ford, and even though Roush Racing made an attempt to keep Ford in GTP, those efforts were less than successful. Overall, Porsche dominated the 1987 GTP series with Holbert Racing winning again. Chevrolet, with no wins, tallied only seventy-nine points, second to Porsche's 305, and Jaguar earned seventy-six points and two wins. The thrill of GTP racing had lost some of its luster.

The new Corvette GTP cars were about one hundred pounds lighter and they were quick—setting four poles and three race fastest laps that season. But they rarely went the distance and scored no wins. Frustrations began when qualifying for the 24-Hours of Daytona; the engine blew just as Van Der Merwe began his qualifying run for the pole. He coasted to a stop with no chance to extend his consecutive poles. He had, however, posted the

*(opposite)* **West Palm Beach, April 24, 1988, was the last race for #22 (HU-8610/02) as a Turbo-V6. Sarel Van Der Merwe and Arie Luyendyk were teamed but the car lasted only six laps. Car #52, (HU-8710/01) in its second race was originally built as a 6.0-liter V8. Elliott Forbes-Robinson and Bobby Rahal started sixth and handled the car excellently, only to be sidelined late in the race.**

*(below)* **"Smokin' Sarel" and Elliott Forbes-Robinson with friend at Laguna Seca.**

A

A. Porsche's legacy in world class long distance endurance racing began in the 1950s. The 906 of 1966 (flat-six) led to this 962 (turbo flat-six). Introduced in 1984, the 3-liter, 680 HP 962 Porsches won 34 of 52 races entered by mid-1987, a formidable reputation.

B. Similar to the 956 in design and layout, except the driver was positioned farther back in the car, the 962's first win in IMSA was Al Holbert's victory at Mid-Ohio, June 10, 1984.

(opposite) Four years running, Porsche 962 won the Sebring 12-Hours, finishing one-two-three. This is Brian Redman in '87; he finished third.

B

B

A

C

third fastest qualifying time of the sixty-nine entrants. With the engine changed, the new power plant developed problems, and a third engine was installed. In a valiant show of dedication, the team had the car on the starting grid, and after a dozen laps, Van Der Merwe was leading, only to run out of gas on the back straight on the twenty-eighth lap. Coasting in for fuel, the car was topped off and went back out, but after 255 laps, around midnight, Bundy and Van Der Merwe were out with a broken drive shaft. Porsche went on to take its eleventh consecutive 24-Hours of Daytona victory (Holbert, Bell, Robinson, and Unser, Jr. made up the team), and Nissan was moving up.

From the opening round at Daytona, the GTP season was fiercely contested. In 1987, lap times dropped by about three seconds overall. Three major changes were introduced by the Hendrick Corvette team: Chevrolet introduced a new generation electronic engine management system; late in the year a new Corvette GTP with V8 power came on the scene; and also late in the year, an active suspension was fitted to a new car.

The DNF at Daytona, a not running finish at Miami after 103 laps, and no entry at Sebring resolved the question of the Corvette GTP's endurance capability and left open the question of sprint capability. Then, in the fourth round at Road Atlanta, Van Der Merwe re-established the pole potential of the Turbo-V6. As defending champions, he and Bundy built up a fifteen-second lead ahead of the following Nissan and Porsche, then a head gasket blew and sidelined the car. The black and silver cars were now associated with the doom and gloom of bad luck.

At the following race at Riverside—the site of the horrific crash in '86 that destroyed one of the Zakspeed Mustang Probe GTP cars driven by Lyn St. James, the second Hendrick Corvette GTP handled by Bundy (710/01), and the Tullius/Chip Robinson XJR-7 Jaguar—Van Der Merwe was on the pole. His car showed superiority by setting the fastest race lap and establishing the lead on the fourth lap, then on lap 63 a valve spring let go. Bang! Bad luck returned. Elliott Forbes-Robinson gave the Nissan GTP

ZX-Turbo a new track record in qualifying, and although out after twenty laps, the Nissans were looking better and better. The Group A Jaguar team won the race.

In the next race, on a beautiful day at Laguna Seca, the Goodwrench Corvette was gridded third, and Van Der Merwe could easily have been on the pole. He raced to second overall in what could easily have been a win, but minor incidents kept him from the winner's circle. With this high finish, the team thought the cloud had lifted, and looked upon the coming race at Lime Rock with high hopes of victory. However, Chevrolet engineers wanted to thoroughly test the new engine management system, so Lime Rock was bypassed for Mid-Ohio, where the cars delivered similar performances but with better fuel economy.

Shakedown testing at Mid-Ohio was encouraging, and two cars were entered for Van Der Merwe and Bundy in the lead car, along with Michael and John Andretti in the second car. Michael was gridded third and Van Der Merwe fifth. When the throttle sensor on the Andretti car failed, dropping it to eleventh, and a misfire above 7,500 RPM appeared in the lead car, the cloud was still there. Van Der Merwe and Bundy held on for a third overall finish while Geoff Brabham in the Electramotive Nissan GTP ZX-T set both the pole and the race fastest lap. Rahal and Jochen Mass in the Bayside Disposal Porsche 962 led the last seventeen laps to win.

Returning to West Palm Beach as defending champions, the Hendrick team had high hopes for a good race. Unfortunately, the cloud was still with them. After Van Der Merwe set both the pole and the fastest lap—both new records—the in-car radio went out, the engine developed a misfire, the turbo boost suddenly increased dramatically, and the nose of the car was crunched by contact with a Camel Lights car—all at the same time. The worst was yet to come. Van Der Merwe pitted early and the turbo waste gate was adjusted to reduce boost pressure, then Bundy took over. The tight street course provided little room for a car to stop on the course and little visibility for approaching cars. Those two factors figured significantly in

**A. The cockpit of the Corvette GTP was similar to all other cars of its type, simple but functional. One-hand driving while changing gears choreographed with precise footwork became a man-and-machine universe known only to the world's top drivers.**

**B. Race day is the culmination of untold manhours of design, fabrication, building, development, and testing. What race fans see is only the crowning tip of human effort to push the bounds of physics in beautiful cars capable of insane speeds and acceleration.**

**C. Sebring test session, March 1988.**

A. The complex of light but strong materials channels air into respective streams to assist in cooling.

B. Lola chassis construction with the all-aluminum 6.0-liter (366 CID) V8 nestled amidship produced a bellowing *basso profundo* racing car that spoke to the world through open exhaust pipes.

*(below)* Race preparation in the Hendrick Motorsports shop in 1987. Note the large air inlet fan coupled to the turbo. It fed the fuel injection pressure box.

*(opposite)* Chassis number HU-8610/02.

A

B

90

was postponed some six hours for course preparation, but Van Der Merwe set the pole with what
he called "a banzai run." During the race, though, a
fuel feed problem indicated that the cloud of doom
was still with the team. Van Der Merwe switched
over to the backup fuel pump and dropped to
fourth. During the pit stop, Bundy relieved him,
and continued to race on the reserve pump. The car
soon overheated, but it did not fail, and went on to
finish third. Porsche won again.

For Corvette GTP racing fans, the gloomiest day
of the season was in November, when Van Der
Merwe announced that he was leaving the Hendrick
team. His many championships in rally competition had brought him a contract with Audi and
Volkswagen, so he returned home to South Africa to
race the factory cars. The year had been one of endless frustrations and few successes. The final two
races, at Columbus and Del Mar, both Porsche wins,
could have been spectacular turnarounds, but both
were DNFs with the Corvette dead last in the final
race.

The elusive turnaround might have come with
the GM/Lotus-derived active suspension. However,
this high tech development was seen by race organizers and other race teams as a step up in cost and
complexity for no good reason, other than speed.
The computerized system was fully active in that all
sensory inputs, such as driver commands, road sur-
faces, and wheel movements, were analyzed by real-
time computer processing, and adjustments were
made to the hydraulics for maintaining the car in a
stable ride position. Wheel movement and body
movement were decoupled. For instance, body roll
was virtually eliminated in turns, and all road sur-
faces were smoothed out with an interactive system
that continuously positioned wheel movement rela-
tive to traction, maximizing adhesion of the patch of
tire in contact with the road. The nose of the car did
not lift under acceleration, and the tail did not squat.
Driver shake was eliminated, and feedback through
the wheel was no more than what the front tires
were doing, no bounce, no jounce, no jitter. Free
sprung tire movement was virtually eliminated,
which meant that wheel well arches could be

reduced. Pre-set forces in spring, tire, and suspension movement were controlled so that movements
such as pothole bumps and washboard jitters were
dampened, rather than allowed to freely seek natural
positions. Higher G-loads in cornering were easily
achieved with reduced driver effort, and sudden rear
end breakaway was virtually eliminated. Steering
became casual. With this invention, the topography
of the race world would change.

The system was pioneered by Peter Wright of
Group Lotus in England, which was owned by
General Motors at the time. The system was intended primarily for Formula One racing. By the time
the Corvette GTP was fitted with the system, more
than a dozen sets of components had been sold as
the Lotus Excel Mark III active system. Its software
was capable of monitoring sixty-seven separate
parameters and making over one thousand changes
each second to the 3,000 PSI hydraulic pumps for
suspension control. The Mark III was, however, just
the precursor of the Mark IV system intended for
production.

In testing the active suspension Corvette GTP at
Columbus, Van Der Merwe noticed an immediate
improvement in the handling characteristics of the
car. He commented: "There is no doubt in my mind
that this is a far superior system to conventional suspension setups. In the short span of ten practice
laps, a team should be able to gain the optimum
setup for any track with this computerized active
suspension system."

In Columbus on October 4, 1987, the Hendrick
Motorsports GM Goodwrench Corvette GTP (8610/02)
made history as the first American race car to run
with an active suspension system. In fully developed
form, the system would prove to be a revolutionary
advance in automobiles when controlled by high-
speed hydraulics with multichannel computers and
real-time processor technology.

John Pierce, Chevrolet Special Projects Engineer,
stated, "Racing is the ideal place to showcase this
type of advanced technology and GM's involvement
with it. In engineering significance, the evolution of
the active suspension has been described as equiva-
lent to reinventing the wheel."

**A. The pump used to charge the Lotus-designed active suspension.**

**B. Electronic union of the active suspension components came together just over the transaxle.**

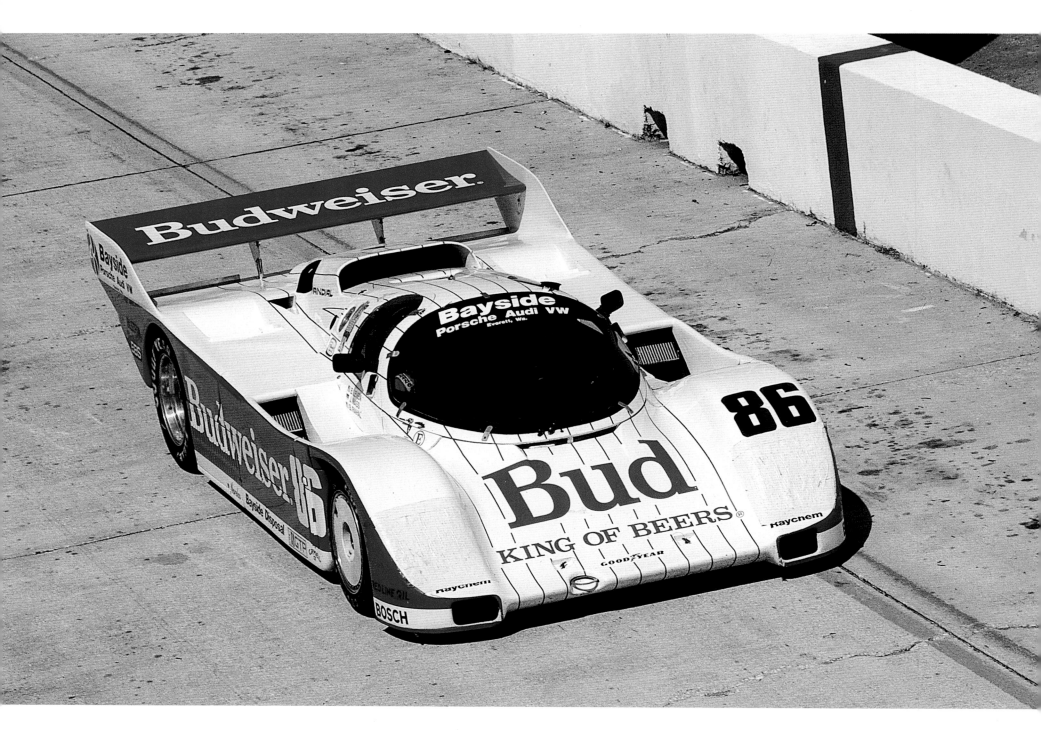

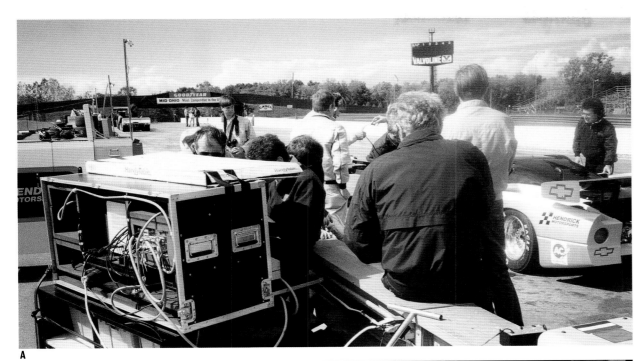

A

B

*(opposite)* The Sebring 12-Hours of 1987 was a duel between Porsche 962s; Jochen Mass and Bobby Rahal won in this car, a close race against the Al Holbert and Chip Robinson Columbia Crest entry.

A. Testing the active suspension car (HU-8612/03) at Mid-Ohio in 1987.

B. Porsche's 962 single turbo flat-six engine evolved from the production 911 engine of 1966 and became IMSA's most successful racing engine.

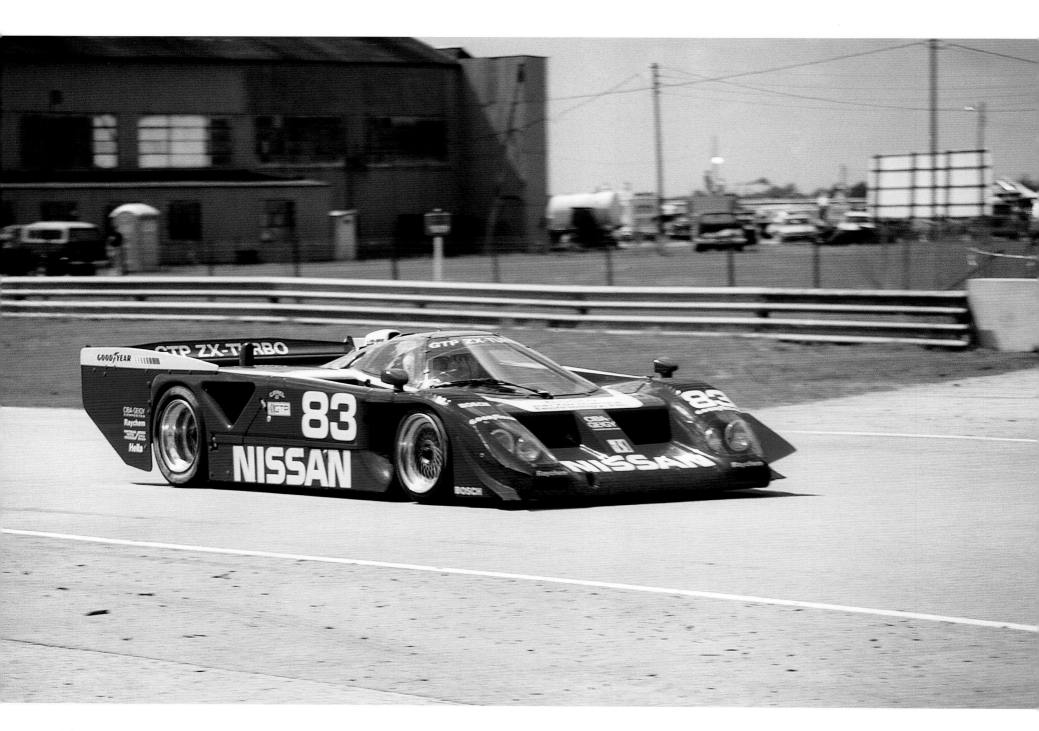

A

B

(*opposite*) Geoff Brabham in the Electramotive Nissan entry won nine of twelve races and the championship in '88 and nine of fifteen races in '89 for a consecutive championship, then followed that with five wins in '90 for his third straight championship.

A. What began as a Lola T-810 chassis powered by a production based Turbo-V6 engine was steadily refined into an all-conquering racing machine.

B. With all the restrictions imposed by IMSA, the turbocharged Nissan engine was claimed by its competitors to produce over 1,000 HP. It developed 780 HP at 8,000 RPM in endurance racing form.

Rick Hendrick added, "What we see in this car today is definitive proof that racing does contribute to expanding the frontiers of automotive development. Chevrolet and GM deserve tremendous credit for bringing this about."

During the race at Columbus, the first scheduled pit stop produced a surprise; when the car was jacked up, the wheels went with the car, just as the computer commanded. Van Der Merwe had to shut off the car to let the wheels settle so that tire changes could proceed. Then, re-entering the race, he was at the back of the pack. He quickly worked his way back up to sixth, when a valve in the active system failed. Pitting on the backup system that was not designed to be raced, the car was retired. The Lotus active suspension system as fitted to the Corvette GTP was designed for Formula One cars, and with one thousand pounds more weight in the GTP car, further refinements were required.

At Del Mar for the last race, two cars were entered, neither with active suspensions. Gridded sixth, Van Der Merwe quickly moved up a position at the start, then tagged the wall in an effort to avoid a collision coming into Turn 3. Damaged bodywork forced retirement of the car after just one lap, and just seventeen laps later, Bundy—who gridded seventh—retired as well.

"All in all," said Van Der Merwe, "a rather pathetic ending to a disappointing season."

The 1987 IMSA GTP season provided highs and lows for several teams, but the aging Porsche 962 chassis design dating from 1982 was still king of the hill. Well proven and durable, even with continual rule changes giving competitors distinct advantages, the Porsches dominated the 1987 season so thoroughly that GTP racing was little more than a Porsche show. However, just as the 1986 season and its terrific competition emerged from the previous year's evolution, the 1988 season grew from seeds sown in '87, along with handsomely increased purses and year-end bonuses. And what a year it was.

The Nissan ZX-Turbo GTP cars in the hands of Geoff Brabham handed the German cars their first consistent defeats, eight in a row out of nine wins by Brabham in the fourteen-race schedule. And the

entry of Tom Walkinshaw Racing XJR-9 IMSA GTP Jaguars to a three-year involvement with IMSA sparked enormous interest in the series.

The 7-liter V12-powered TWR Jags with Silk Cut sponsorship swept the 1987 Sports Prototype World Championship, winning eight of ten races, and captured both the Drivers and Manufacturers Championships. IMSA rules for 1988 were slightly different than Group C regulations, most significantly the engine displacement limit of 6-liters. Otherwise, the new GTP Jags were modest evolutions of the XJR-8. During December of that year, the TWR shop south of Chicago had two cars successfully testing at Talladega and Daytona and creating quite a stir among GTP enthusiasts. The new Jaguars also created another tire war by racing on Dunlops, the first major entry in the IMSA series for the brand.

Bob Tullius entered his older Group 44 Jaguar with Goodyears, and Bob Wollek started the 24-Hours of Daytona from the pole in the BFGoodrich Porsche 962 due to Mario Baldi's fastest qualifying lap in the car. But even with Brian Redman's talents as co-driver in the Porsche, the three TWR Castrol Jaguars in line from the outside pole told the story by ending the Porsche streak of eleven wins at Daytona. The Jags finished one-two-three to great fanfare and celebration.

Baldi's solo qualifying lap in the Porsche was close to Van Der Merwe's record set in the 3.4-liter Turbo-V6 Corvette GTP the year before, but the Lola-Chevy record stood. The Corvette GTP made its first 1988 appearance at Miami, the second race in the series. Two cars were entered, one with Turbo-V6 power and a new car (8710-01) with V8 power. By May, the V6 car (8610-02) was converted over to V8 as well, and for the duration of Corvette GTP racing, cars were V8s.

The lineup of Hendrick Motorsports drivers was a sterling cast of greats: Elliott Forbes-Robinson and David Hobbs in the V6 car, Number 22, along with Van Der Merwe and Bobby Rahal in the V8 car, Number 52. The cars were, unfortunately, not competitive even though gridded tenth and twelfth at the start. The Jaguars, Porsches, and Nissans posted superior times, and the cloud remained over the

**(opposite) Like the BMW GTP, the Mustang Probe engine was a turbocharged inline-4 constructed of aluminum. At 650-plus HP from 2.1-liters (129 CID), its top speed was 230 MPH. The car weighed 1,980 pounds. Designed by Paul Brown of Zakspeed USA, it was driven by three-time Le Mans winner Klaus Ludwig and Doc Bundy.**

Hendrick team. A broken shift lever put Number 22 out of contention on lap 15, but the car returned to the race after an hour of repairs. Number 22 was running at the finish but completed only seventy-seven laps, well down from the 124 laps posted by the winning Porsche. A broken throttle cable sidelined Number 52 after fifty-four laps, and the new season began where the previous season left off.

The brightest spot in the 1988 season was the excellent run at Watkins Glen with Van Der Merwe and Forbes-Robinson. Starting tenth, they finished third in chassis number 8710/01 fitted with a new short tail body and two-element wing. The last entry for a Hendrick Motorsports Goodwrench Corvette GTP was, fittingly, with Van Der Merwe behind the wheel at Del Mar, a track he did not like. He qualified third and completed only twenty-four laps. Bobby Rahal in the second car (8610/02, which was retubbed and configured as a short tail V8 car) was gridded eleventh at the start and finished fifth. Despite officially leaving the Hendrick team after the 1987 season, Van Der Merwe had driven in all but one race entered in '88.

At the end of Hendrick Corvette GTP racing, with all of its frustrations, crew chief Ken Howes thought the cars could still be competitive; they just needed development.

A

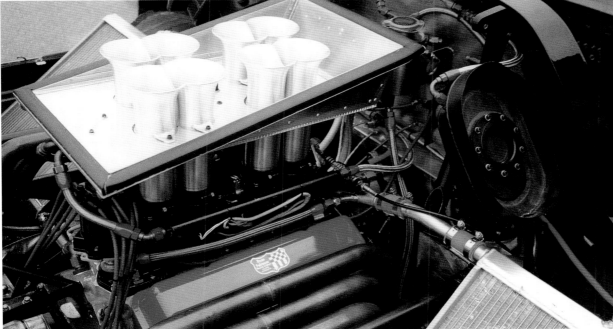

B

**(opposite) Sears Point, August 1988. In short tail form and V8-powered, HU-8710/01 started eighth and finished ninth with Van Der Merwe and Forbes-Robinson. Two months later, the Hendrick Motorsports GM Goodwrench Corvette GTP team withdrew from competition.**

**A. The TWR Jaguar GTP engine of 6.0-liters; over 700 HP.**

**B. Ryan Falconer's engine work in V8 form was not as powerful as the Turbo-V6, but lap times were about the same due to quicker response and low end torque.**

# KEN HOWES

**"We won two races, Road Atlanta and West Palm Beach. In 1987 we really had the bit between our teeth. We figured we were going to do well."**

➤ At the time, 1988, I had been racing for twenty-two years. I'm from South Africa and raced there or worked in racing since I was eighteen years old. It seems like, you name it, and I have done it somewhere. Mainly single seater cars, Formula One, F-2, and Formula Atlantic. Through the '60s, and in fact right to the '70s, we ran up-to-date, current Formula One cars. We started with a Lotus 49, and a few years later bought a Lotus 72, and we ran those for several years in the early '70s.

The next year, 1974, we ran a Lotus 72 again in the Formula One championship with the same driver, Ian Scheckter, and finished second in the South African Championship that year. Then in 1975 we ran a Tyrrell 007 and came in second again. We won the championship in 1976, '77, '78, and '79, at which time we got a little tired of it. I was team manager, and we were building cars, building engines, and racing all the time. The most people that I ever employed at one time was four. It is always a lot of hard work, no matter how many people you have, and we are still busting a gut somehow with the GTP Corvette.

In 1980, we went into a GTO type of racing in South Africa. The regulations are very similar, and technically, we won that championship. We won enough races to theoretically win the championship, but through the year we had an ongoing struggle with the regulations and legality of the car. In a sense, we got conned when they let us race, because they needed us, but we knew that they were ultimately going to do us in. They did.

That was kind of a low point in my career, and we all got a little disillusioned with it. At that point, Ian retired and I kept the workshop going but we really didn't run a team. So, 1981 was a little bit of a nothing year, just finding ways to pay the rent. Then in 1982, the championship changed a little where the cars had progressed to where they were really Formula Two chassis but we used Mazda rotary engines, and I ran a car for Graham Duxbury. We ended third or fourth in the championship.

Then in 1983 we ran a two-car team and enticed Ian Scheckter back out of retirement. We ran a March chassis with Mazda rotary power.

*(opposite)* **At Road Atlanta in April 1987, chassis HU-8610/01 was fitted with a new, stronger tub. Van Der Merwe set a new absolute track record (1:11.638) in the car and was on the pole.**

A. HU-710/01 being rebuilt.

B. For the first race for chassis HU-8610/01 (Charlotte, May 18, 1986), improved over the original T-710 design, the crew used the Hendrick NASCAR shop. Van Der Merwe and Bundy finished fourth overall in the Spirit of Charlotte.

We then won that championship in 1983 and again in 1984 with Ian.

That is when my life went upside down, because early in 1984, Kreepy Krauly, a manufacturer of swimming pool cleaners, decided to set up their own team in America, GTP, and approached me and asked if I would run it for them. Well, I had a contract to run this Formula Two team, and I was in a bind. I spoke to the people in South Africa, and thought about it, and went to our sponsors and explained what was going on. They said, "Well, we think that you are in good enough shape. Why don't you do both?"

So, in 1984 I ran two teams, one in South Africa and one in America. I commuted, literally. I would be in America for two weeks, and in South Africa for two weeks. That was tough, but we had a reasonably successful year with that GTP car. We won the Daytona 24-Hours race with Sarel Van Der Merwe, Tony Martin, and Graham Duxbury, and we won again at Lime Rock. That was with a March 84G that we bought from Al Holbert. He had used it in 1983.

My thoughts at the time were that we were having to start up a new team in a strange country. I needed a car that had some kind of potential and one that the problems had been solved in. I didn't need to start out with everything against me. We ran Andial Porsche engines, and to this day I am very good friends with Alvin Springer of Andial.

In 1985, I decided that I could no longer commute back and forth. I decided to come to America full time, and run the Kreepy Krauly team. We planned to do the full season, but after the 24-Hours race at Daytona, politics got involved and, effectively, Kreepy Krauly withdrew. What happened was an anti-South African lobby in Florida was looking for publicity for their cause, and we were using essentially South African money and had South African drivers and a South African team manager. They approached the Miami organizers for permission to have an anti-South African demonstration at the Miami Grand Prix. That was the beginning of it, and there was a lot of bad stuff flying around. They then threatened to picket Kreepy Krauly's retail outlets. The company was not big enough to fight some-

thing like that, and we decided to withdraw from the Miami Grand Prix. At that point Kreepy Krauly looked at their involvement and decided to withdraw their support.

They were good with me personally. They tided me over and left me here with this shop in Indianapolis. We were based in Atlanta in 1984, then we moved to Indianapolis, and have been happy here. At that time in 1985 things were looking bleak. I managed to keep the doors open for a little while. Kreepy Krauly had agreed to sponsor a trip to Le Mans, so we converted one of our race cars to Group C regulations and did the race at Le Mans in 1985, but we didn't do very well. Fortunately, we were able to sell the car in Europe and get some of the money back.

Then about that time, this project with Rick Hendrick and Chevrolet came along. In 1984, there had been a lot of talk around that Chevrolet had this car and was looking for a team to run it. In 1984, John Pierce of Chevrolet Special Products had come to various racetracks talking with people. Everybody knew that this project was out there somewhere, and of course a lot of people were chasing it. We had spoken to John Pierce, and he knew who we were. I never thought any more of it. When our problems became known, this was around March of 1985, I was thinking, I have Le Mans to do and after that I don't know what's going to happen.

Out of the blue, John Pierce called me and said, "I hear that you have some problems. What is happening?" I told him, and he gave me the number of Rick Hendrick. I phoned him, and that was the beginning of this project.

Chevrolet had approached Rick Hendrick to get involved. He was very interested but his background was NASCAR. He really didn't know what IMSA was all about. It was almost a perfect match. Rick had the car and Chevrolet's support and here in Indianapolis was an IMSA team that didn't have anything to do. Rick paid us to do some testing initially, because no one knew if the car was going to be competitive, as it had been lying under covers. The car was built by Lola in England, commissioned by Chevrolet.

Chevrolet had gone into this project where their stylists and aerodynamics people had an idea of what a Corvette GTP should look like. Initially, a body was built in Detroit based on a Lola T-600. Aerodynamic tests were done in the wind tunnel at that point, and Lola was commissioned to build a better car with that body style. That car was built, and the V6 engine was developed with Ryan Falconer's involvement. Nothing really came of it. One story I have heard was that there was a management change at Chevrolet, and the new person really wasn't interested. When I first saw the car, it was in Detroit under a cover and had been lying like that for about a year. It had been tested a few times, briefly, but nothing had come of it.

Rick Hendrick and Chevrolet got together. So, through September, we were paid by Rick Hendrick to test the car and solve some of the problems, but it was fairly obvious that the car was going to be competitive. At that point Hendrick decided to enter a few races. I was thankful for it, because it helped me keep the doors open.

Our first race was at Road America in 1985, and we qualified reasonably well, but had engine trouble. I think the next time we raced was at Daytona, and again the car was competitive, but the engine program really wasn't up to speed. At that point, things had gone well enough that Chevrolet got serious about it. At the beginning of 1986, I was able to put a good team together. We continued in 1985 with that first car, and in May of 1986 we received the first of our newer cars. Lola built another car for a V8 engine, and that car, somewhere down the line, was sold.

The Lola T-710 chassis was tidied up some. Then, in June of 1986, we received our second car. At Riverside that year, Doc Bundy crashed the original car very badly and effectively demolished it. We did resurrect it here one winter, and it is now a show car, but it is not really suitable to race.

The three cars we had in 1987 all evolved from those two cars that we took over in 1986. We kept replacing them and updating them with fair success. We won two races, Road Atlanta and West Palm Beach. In 1987 we really had the bit between our

teeth. We figured we were going to do well, but we ended up with a lot of engine problems. It was mainly the electronic management system.

Chevrolet, in the winter of 1986–87, developed their first-generation electronic management system, and it seems like that killed us. So, 1987 was a pretty bleak year, but we showed promise. We qualified well but never were reliable and really came away with nothing to show for the year.

For 1988, Chevrolet had a new electronic management system that they called the Generation 2, which turned out to be very good and very reliable. But the IMSA regulations changed, and they put a restrictor on turbocharged engines. That took away the one big advantage that the V6 had, which was very, very good horsepower.

The good horsepower hid a lot of sins. It made the average chassis look very good because we could just out-power anybody, but reliability problems plagued us. The restrictor took away the one advantage we had, so what we ended up with was a car that was getting old and, after the restrictor plate rule, down on power.

In 1985, we were probably qualifying with somewhere around 900 horsepower, racing at well over 800 horsepower with the V6. That continued through 1986 and 1987, qualifying at around 850 to 900. What the restrictor did was bring us down to just a little over 700 horsepower. That's a big jump. I began thinking that if the normally aspirated V8 could make 680, that seemed to be a good trade off. Complexity was down, it didn't have throttle lag, and it had a good power band. The V6 had a very narrow power band.

The basic design of the car was laid out in late 1983 or early 1984, so by 1988 it was starting to show. The V6 engine was no longer a good combination, and IMSA regulations had encouraged normally aspirated V8 engines by this time. We felt like it was time to investigate that, so over the winter of 1987 and 1988 we assembled one car with a V8 engine. We continued with the V6, but took both cars to every racetrack we went to and did a lot of testing. It was apparent that the V8 car was just about as good. It didn't have the throttle lag and

wasn't difficult to drive. It seemed like it was going to be reliable, but we were still a small team, and trying to run two cars with two very different engine layouts began to show. We weren't doing anything well. We were just doing both jobs badly.

We then decided to just concentrate on the V8 development, and it looked promising. We built up a third car with the V8, so we now had two V8 cars, and we put the V6 aside, hoping that development would continue on it, but it never did. ➤

*(opposite)* **At Road Atlanta, Van Der Merwe led the first quarter of the race and set the fastest lap of the race (1:14.540), but the car lasted only fifty-one laps.**

the 917/10 engine had its own turbocharger and the overall design was another technical masterpiece, another landmark achievement by Porsche. It was the first real application of turbocharging to racing and produced an overwhelming power plant.

For the 1973 Can-Am season, the Roger Penske team had two new magnesium frame 917/30 Porsches for driver Mark Donohue. In top form, these cars were widely regarded as the ultimate in racing and delivered up to 1,200 HP, depending on boost. Donohue raced the famed Sunoco-sponsored Porsche-Audi car and dominated every event. He won the last six races of the season in the new 917/30 to take the Can-Am championship with a point total nearly double that of George Follmer, who was in second place.

Porsche won eight of eight races that year with the net effect of strangling the competitive spirit of teams who faced them. By 1974, even with rule changes favoring anything but the Porsche, the once vibrant and exciting Can-Am series became a dismal failure and fizzled out mid-year, largely because the 917/30 had a tested top speed of 257 MPH and handled so well through corners that its lap times virtually insured victory.

The dual turbocharged Porsche 917/30 engine at 1,200 HP developed 222.2 HP per liter. That was the mark that stood until Falconer surpassed it with the Corvette GTP Turbo-V6. When compared to the complex Porsche engine with its four valves per cylinder and dual overhead cams in a flat-twelve, air-cooled configuration, the water-cooled 3.4-liter Chevrolet at just 900 HP developed 265 HP per liter. At peak power, developing 1,200 HP in qualifying form, the Falconer V6 produced 353 HP per liter. That mark is likely to stand for quite a long time.

Chevrolet's lead engine man on the Corvette GTP, Richard Johnson, and development engineer Bill Howell produced equipment for the internal cam pushrod engine that reliably handled 9,000 RPM in sustained racing conditions. For the crankshaft/piston assembly, valve train, and associated internals to perform under stresses of the magnitude developed at 9,000 RPM is a most remarkable achievement, the sort of achievement that enabled Sarel Van Der

Merwe to capture one pole position and track record after another. For the same hardware to produce and handle 900-plus HP in racing conditions of three hundred to five hundred miles in length is also a truly remarkable achievement.

As is often the case with excessive power in a racing car, faults were often masked. Beginning with the T-600 and its diving problem that was never solved, the Lola chassis—as late as the T-8710 GTP car—needed refinement to become as well balanced as the Porsches. While the Electramotive team was making their Lola chassis competitive, and eventually building chassis that eclipsed those of the Porsches, the Corvette GTP team was saddled with one compromise after another that led to disappointing results.

However, the purpose of the effort from Chevrolet's perspective was development of new concepts applicable to production cars. That objective will forever stand in stark conflict with the objectives of a racing team. Chevrolet may have achieved its engineering goals, but the sad fact remains that what could have come from the Corvette GTP program in terms of celebrated racing history was lost.

Unlike the highly successful Ford racing program of the 1960s, in which the goal first and foremost was winning races to establish engineering excellence, the Corvette GTP came only tantalizingly close to what it could have achieved. All the ingredients were in place for a Chevrolet championship car.

Eric Broadley had been instrumental in the original Ford GT40 program of 1963 and learned sufficiently from his Lola GT and the Ford effort to design and market his Chevrolet-powered Lola T-70, which was highly successful by 1966. John Surtees won the first Can-Am Challenge Cup championship in a Chevy-powered T-70. Later, Mark Donohue drove the Penske Sunoco Special Lola-Chevrolets to the United States Road Racing Championship in 1967 and '68—the same series that Al Holbert's father, Bob Holbert, won in 1963.

As he was with the Corvette GTP twenty years later, Carl Haas was the importer of all the Lolas sold in this country. But unlike his lack of involvement with the GTP cars, he was directly associated with the Penske effort in the '60s. By the time GTP racing

came on strong in the early 1980s, Broadley had another success in the Brian Redman-inspired T-600. Along with this series of Lola cars, the Chevrolet-powered March GTP cars proved to be championship caliber as well.

Thus, all the ingredients were in place for a Chevrolet champion in the Lola-Chevrolet Corvette GTP; the engine had the power, the chassis had the potential, the drivers were superb, the team was of top professional caliber, and the car showed its potential brilliantly, but only in flashes of victory rather than the sustained success needed to build a lasting legacy. The obvious question—why wasn't the Corvette GTP the success it should have been?—will remain forever unanswered.

Two wins and a string of poles do not make a lasting tradition, and even though Ford's world championships and Le Mans victories occurred about three decades ago, Ford fans and racing historians continually retell the great legacy of Ford domination in world class racing. And Ford Motor Company continues to benefit from this positive exposure in magazine features and other media coverage, while the Corvette GTP will be remembered largely by disappointed fans who believed that great success was within the grasp of the Chevrolet team.

Even though record books may not illustrate the potential of the Corvette GTP, it was a truly magnificent racing car with all the ingredients to become a true legend. As the most powerful GTP car of its time, and certainly a technical achievement of historic importance, the GM Goodwrench Corvette GTP will remain forever an inspiration in the imaginations of the millions of Chevrolet racing fans everywhere who saw the cars race, and an excellent example of great expectations turned to paradise lost.

**(opposite) Nissan ZX-Turbos dominated IMSA GTP racing from 1988 through '91.**

ended up running the other car, which also had one of my engines, the 6-liter V8 in a T-600. He was leading the race when a horrendous downpour occurred; he hit a puddle and slid off the course. Holbert ended up winning the race. The irony was that Holbert was running one of my engines in his March-Chevy. That race showed that the turbo had the potential. Some things happened during the year, and the association of Interscope and Chevrolet stopped in '83.

We still didn't have much hardware to work with. Basically, we had two long blocks. I continued to work with Ongais; we tried the 24-Hours race at Daytona, which was way premature for the engine. What stopped us in that race was that the exhaust system broke and started melting the magnesium bell housing.

The word had gotten around that GM was building a new car. I knew about it because I had been working with Eric Broadley at Lola since the early 1960s. It was a Lola that John Pierce, Piggins, me, and a few others were working on. I knew the deal was coming up for 1984, so I went over to Lola Cars with Pierce, and we started running the first GTP car. The very first time it was on a track was at Goodwood. That was the first time the car rolled a wheel, and Jonathan Palmer drove it.

We had to go back to a single turbo instead of twin turbos, and we were running fairly conservative boost but were still getting about 650, 700 horsepower, in that range. The engines were based on production castings but were heavy-duty blocks that allowed us to go to larger bore. Production blocks would not permit that increase in bore. They were Chevrolet castings referred to as "Bow Tie" equipment. They also made aluminum cylinder heads for us, but IMSA required us to run iron blocks.

In testing, I could tell that the car was far from being right; we had starter problems, we had heating problems, and if you ran the car for several laps and didn't pull the body off, it would burn, even in freezing cold. So, there was a lot to be done to this good-looking car. It was just a basic starting place.

Finally, the car was brought over from England and was sort of parked. I bitched and moaned to General Motors and got them to let me bring the car out to my shop in California to make it a runner.

I hired people whom I had worked with, such as Jim Chapman of Jim Chapman Development and John Bright, to work with me. We did some cooling modifications to the turbo and some other modifications. Then, because of past friendships, I got Mario Andretti to come out and test the car for a couple of sessions. I got Al Unser, Jr. for a couple more tests, and Al Unser, Sr. as well. So, I had some good test drivers.

When the car finally began to show potential, GM made a deal with Rick Hendrick to take the car on and campaign it. Rick came out and met with me, and we had a long talk about where we were going with the program. I did the engines right up to the end. It was a good relationship that worked very well.

There were several V6-powered cars—the GTP Nissan, Buick, and the Corvette—but we got the first win with the V6. That meant a lot to me. In retrospect, a lot of the engine development should have been a different way. We won our first race with mechanical fuel injection, then GM decided to build their own electronic injection system. That set us back five years. They don't want to hear that part of the story, but it really did. That disappointed me because when the injection failed, I took the hit for it. But that was the learning curve. We started out with the engine at about 600 horsepower and ended up with almost 1,200 in single turbo form. We ran that engine in the car at well over 1,000 horsepower.

Sarel Van Der Merwe was an excellent driver. I really admired him, and we are still good friends. He was a hell of a driver, afraid of nothing. Although updates were made to the chassis, we were running a 1984 car that had an inherent problem: it never put its power down well. So we kept making more and more horsepower, and Sarel could qualify the car making banzai runs, but when the racing started, he would burn the rear tires off. The biggest problem was that Goodyear favored the Porsche 962 because more of them were running. We actually needed a special tire, but that was not to be. We literally had too much power for the tires. When the program finally got going with Rick Hendrick, I had eight V6 engines in the system. When the engine's potential became known, we were required to

reduce displacement from 209 to 183 cubic inches, as were the other competitors.

Sarel was on the pole at Daytona in '86 for the 24-Hours, but we had to withdraw the car. What happened was that on the morning of the race, Wally Dallenbach, one of the backup drivers, went out to take a couple of shakedown laps, then came in saying there was a vibration in the car. It had been smooth all along, so I got the crew to pull the undertray, which they were not happy doing, then I crawled under the car to look around. The front main web was coming out, blown. The crankshaft was literally being supported by the timing chain. I went to Rick and told him we couldn't start. So, we made an announcement that the car had a vibration and we didn't have time to find and correct it, and withdrew in the interest of safety.

That was the iron block. With the power up so high, we were stressing the block, so I redesigned the bottom end and came up with a girdle-type pan arrangement which would allow us to run upwards of 1,000 horsepower without a block failure. When we went to the aluminum block, I did the same type of girdle arrangement and we never had a bottom end failure after that. That was in 1986.

The GTP Corvette was an interesting program in the midst of a lot of development. Nissan was right in there, Buick, too, and for all the effort that Buick put into their program with dual car teams, they never had the success that we had. For instance, when we were at Watkins Glen, a Buick went out and turned 198 MPH down the back straight where they timed the cars. Sarel went out and turned 205 and said, "That will hold them for a while. If we need to, we'll go quicker." That record stood until a couple of years ago. There was no interchange with Buick; they were the competition, and they were strong. It was dog-eat-dog, a war between Joe Negre at Buick and Herb Fischel at Chevrolet.

Then BMW came into it, and the racing got to be fun. They were definitely a formidable force that raised the ante. From my standpoint, engine builder races engine builder, driver races driver, manufacturer races manufacturer. Up to the point that Chevrolet went to the electronic fuel injection, we were doing

pretty well. I could build engines mechanically, but afterwards, I was strapped to their electronics. I wanted to go with what existed and was known, but they wanted to go with their system because they wanted the General Motors connection. That was the only place we had a disagreement.

The primary competition at that time was the Holbert team in the Porsche. They were winning because they had so much knowledge of racing and so much knowledge of the 962 and its engine with Holbert's Andial engine people. Power-wise, we had them covered, but we had to make the car last. That was the shortcoming of the car.

The move to the V8 was said to improve things, but I thought it was a mistake. We got into a controversy about why the car didn't handle well. They said the V6 engine came on too severely, and the driver kept wanting more and more horsepower. I kept giving them what they wanted, and by then we were just getting to the point that the electronic waste gates were beginning to work like they should have. The reason was that the car didn't put its power down well, so when the power came on, it made a hell of a transition. They claimed that all those problems would be solved with the V8, so I built a couple of V8s, and Rick's shop built a couple. I think they ended up with six of those engines. The V8s ran very well, all of them, but the Turbo-V6 still had the advantage. What they found out with the V8 was that the car still did not put its power down. So they began thinking that the V8 wasn't the answer, but kept on with it. If you look at the records, you'll find that Nissan kept on with the V6 and kicked butt. Then the Toyotas went on from there.

You simply can't equate turbo and non-turbo engines, it won't work. The turbo can make the power, the V8 can't. By then, the GTP Corvette was passed by, regardless of the engine. It needed a new chassis. Nissan proved that. The Lola had served its time, and there were newer cars coming in while we were still flogging a dead horse.

We went out of races for blown tires, wheel bearings, crap that should never have happened. If the car didn't finish, few people were concerned with why it didn't finish and claimed it was fragile. I believe that Chevrolet got to the point that they wanted their identification back, and they didn't want it known that outside people were doing the work. I enjoyed the program, but in late '87 we were getting into a political area that I did not like. With an increasingly less competitive car, everyone was blaming everyone else for failures. We had a great group of guys working on this project, but it got to the point that it was very uncomfortable, and I didn't want to be a part of it any more. Right at the end of '87, I decided that I was out.

There were a lot of politics in racing back then. For instance, I took the engine from the GTP car and stuck it in a GTO car, the Protofab Camaro. We made a huge mistake at Watkins Glen; we were backpeddling and still broke the lap record by about two seconds. That brought even more restrictions; we had to downsize the engine to 2.5-liters. We showed too much, and were being restricted out of racing.

Overall, though, the GTP Corvette was a lot of fun and should have won a lot more races than it did. We accomplished a lot more with a lot less than people realize. Most people might assume that this was a massive factory effort. It wasn't. For my part, I had total control over the engine, how to make the power and how to make it last, other than the electronic fuel injection. That was Chevrolet's. I thought it was quite an accomplishment to see the V6 engine go from 600 horsepower in the beginning to 1,200. As a two-valve production-based engine, it was a highly stressed piece, and still was very reliable, given what we had to work with. ➤

**(opposite) The cooling system, consisting of two giant radiators, was barely sufficient for the Turbo-V6, but more than adequate for the V8.**

# GORDON BARRETT

**"With the turbocharged V6 engine, the Corvette GTP was not a smooth car to drive. It was in fact a harsh, severe kind of car because of the amount of power the V6 engine made and how quickly the power would increase over a very short RPM range."**

➤ I was fortunate to have been involved in the Corvette GTP program starting in January of 1986. That was the beginning of a three-year racing contract between Chevrolet and Hendrick Motorsports and GM Goodwrench. It was an exciting time in IMSA GTP racing because there were several manufacturers supporting teams, specifically Chevrolet, Buick, Ford, Jaguar, Nissan, BMW, and Porsche. In addition there were some very well run private teams, mostly using 962 Porsches.

My background for this type of work is that I have a Bachelor of Science degree in mechanical engineering from Carnegie-Mellon University. I worked for Rockwell International in Detroit as a design engineer primarily with brakes and axles used on trucks and off-road vehicles. After a couple of years I realized that I wanted more than to just sit in an office and generate numbers. An opportunity arose to own a race car, and I quickly became involved in the Can-Am series in 1970. We ran a McLaren M6B with an aluminum big-block Chevy in that year and in 1971 for driver Tom Dutton. Then

with the help of two engineers I had met at that time, I was able to get a job with an Indy car team in 1972. From then through 1985 I worked mostly for small teams that built their own Indy cars. That was what I was most interested in doing, the engineering and construction of Indy cars. During those years I was involved with and responsible for the construction of fourteen Indy cars. In the 1980s that work was coming to an end in Indianapolis, with all the building being done in England, primarily by March and Penske and Lola.

A friend had gone to work for the Hendrick team, and he was my introduction there. Ken Howes was the team manager, and everyone else on the team were people I knew from Indy car racing. The chief mechanic was Laurie Gerrish, an Englishman who had worked for the Penske team for many years. Other team members were Tim Love, Greg Hight, Bobby Hatch, Toby Freeman, and John O'Gara. As the work load increased, Greg Beck, Joe Ward, and Matt Hammond were hired.

*(opposite)* **The Hendrick Motorsports crew checks out the engine during testing.**

B

C

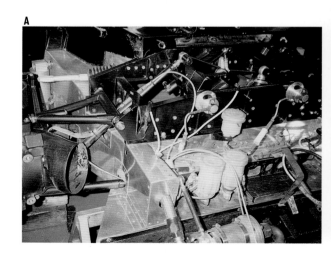

A

My job with the team was mainly doing component engineering and metal fabricating. The cars were built by Lola, but after their arrival, they were in a constant state of development. The main problems we had to address were strength, weight, and airflow through the coolers. We had a permanent battle trying to reduce weight everywhere we could. Chevrolet's corporate connections were very helpful in this area. For instance, they had new windshields made that saved ten pounds each. Airflow was not too good to the side inlets into the water radiator and the turbo intercooler, and with Chevrolet's connection with Harrison, we were able to get lighter and more efficient aluminum core radiators and turbo intercoolers. We also had access to the full-scale General Motors wind tunnel in Warren, Michigan, which was vitally important in improving overall downforce and airflow through the coolers.

The intercooler was a particular problem because of the high boost pressures the car ran to make horsepower. The work of compressing the air heated it to more than 350°F. We generally used an air-to-air intercooler, but once tried one that had a segment that was water-cooled with its own radiator and water pump. Occasionally for qualifying we used a water mist spray bar to further cool the intercooler core. The water was supplied by a windshield washer pump. From what we learned in the wind tunnel we were able to increase aerodynamic downforce by adding slotted louvers to the nose above the front tires and by fastening a lip to the front of the nose bottom. These and other tricks eventually improved the rear wind profile. We also devised some tweaks to improve airflow through the coolers.

In an effort to identify and cure some of the weak areas in the honeycomb aluminum tub, we made a torsional twisting fixture to test the tub. This device was quite successful as we were able to initially improve the torsional strength of the tub by fifty percent, and eventually raised it to over nineteen thousand foot pounds per degree. Trying to keep this car on a diet was tough because these improvements always added some weight. We were able to rework

some other parts to be lighter, such as using a carbon fiber nose bottom to replace the original one of honeycomb aluminum. We changed the plumbing of the oil system to reduce the amount of Aeroquip lines used. Although we always wanted to reduce it, sometimes weight was the price we had to pay to make the car more durable and reliable.

This series of Lola GTP cars was commissioned by Chevrolet, and I believe they were available to anyone who wanted to buy one from Lola. The body styling was done in Detroit, and the chassis were built in England by Lola Cars. The Corvette GTP shape was certainly the most stunning of any sports car racing at the time. All the cars used the Hewland VG or VGC gearbox and were built for either a Chevrolet turbocharged V6 or an injected V8 engine. Of the seven cars built in total, Hendrick Motorsports received five, Lee Racing one, and Peerless Automotive one. The first car was chassis number 710/01, which was initially a test car for Chevrolet. It was tied closely with Ryan Falconer because he was doing the engine development for the turbocharged V6 engine. After being tested in California, the car was placed in storage in Detroit for a short time. Arrangements were then made with Rick Hendrick to race this car, because of his successful association with Chevrolet in stock car racing.

The two most visible Chevrolet engineers involved with the Corvette GTP program were John Pierce and Richard Johnson. John Pierce was the overall engineer in charge of the project and the liaison with Lola Cars. Richard Johnson was in charge of engine development, both Turbo-V6 and injected V8 when we used the latter engine in 1988. Richard's primary focus from 1987 was on design and development of the Chevrolet electronic fuel management system used on both engines.

With the introduction of this system in 1987, I would have to say that the objectives of the Chevrolet engineers began to differ slightly from the objectives of the Hendrick team. While team goals were to run fast and win pole positions and races, the Chevrolet approach was to use every opportunity for a test. If we won races that was great, but their primary objective was development, and the

**A.** Chassis number HU-8610/02 prepared for a test in 1989. Fitted with carbon brakes, strain gauges on front pushrods, and rotation indicators on rocker shafts, data was gathered for improving the design of components.

**B.** A new tub being prepared for installation in chassis 8610/02 after Sebring, 1988.

**C.** Constructed of aluminum sheet metal and honeycomb, the Corvette GTP tub was strong and lightweight. Note the steel bracing in the corners for additional strength.

racing environment provided the sense of urgency that accelerated that process.

Occasionally these two approaches came into conflict. In 1987 at Watkins Glen, Sarel Van Der Merwe had fast times in practice and in group qualifying and for single car qualifying, then Richard Johnson installed a new chip in the fuel management module. Well, the car went out on the track popping and barking and ended up third on the grid. Again in 1987, Sarel was running well at Laguna Seca and leading by a couple of seconds, but was forced into an extra pit stop for fuel because the engine wasn't getting good enough mileage that day; [he] finished second. At Road Atlanta in 1987, it looked like we would have a good race. After starting from the pole and leading for many laps, the electrons in the management system must have become confused because the engine ran lean, became too hot, and then stopped. But we all had to accept that occasional bad days were all part of testing and development, and that was the reason the program existed.

With the questionable reliability of this new fuel management system in 1987, the car's ability to win races was greatly jeopardized. Even though the car could run fast with this system, it only made it into the winner's circle when using the old mechanical fuel injection. But being a Bosch unit, that was definitely Brand-X when viewed from Chevrolet's frame of reference. After constant testing and design improvements, this electronic fuel management system evolved into the one used on the Ilmor Chevrolet Indy car engine. By then it worked very well and contributed to winning many races, but we certainly struggled with it in 1987.

The following year, 1988, we had the benefit of the second-generation management system, but then the Hendrick/Chevrolet V6 program was dealt a severe blow by the IMSA rules. A turbocharger inlet restrictor was required, which reduced the amount of air that could be pumped into the engine. Since we had been using high boost to get high horsepower, this rule hurt us the most. With greatly reduced horsepower from the 3.0-liter Turbo-V6, the decision was made to use a normally aspirated

6.0-liter V8. The power characteristics of the V8 engine made the car much easier to drive, but even this engine did not make competitive horsepower. So that, coupled with our now aging chassis design, caused the 1988 season to be difficult for us—no poles, no wins.

We had high hopes that the contract with Chevrolet could be continued and that we would have a new car design for the 1989 season, but the funding was just not available. So the racing ended for us at the close of the 1988 season. A few of us stayed on, and we continued until early 1990 doing testing for Chevrolet. The objectives were further refinement of the fuel management system and a data acquisition system and conducting engine feasibility tests.

One of the technical highlights of the Corvette GTP program was the use of the Lotus active suspension on one of the cars. A new car was sent from Lola to the Lotus factory and fitted with the active system that was being used on their Formula One cars. The car was tested in England before being brought to our shop in Indianapolis for further development. We tested it at Watkins Glen, Road Atlanta, and Mid-Ohio before entering the race at Columbus in 1988.

Basically, the spring/shock absorber units on the car were replaced by hydraulic cylinders. A special oil pump on the engine kept two accumulator tanks charged with 300 PSI oil that was metered to the hydraulic cylinders by computer-controlled valves. This system, conceived by Peter Wright at Lotus, was very effective but extremely complex and required the assistance of Lotus engineers to run it. An example of its effectiveness is that the car could run laps consistently at track record times in testing at Road Atlanta, with far less than qualifying boost. The technical capabilities of this active system were unbelievable. It could computer control ride height, spring rates, damping characteristics, roll, dive, and squat resistance, and any single parameter could be programmed to be driver adjustable between pre-selected limits. This system was magic!

Unfortunately our race debut with this car was less than spectacular, only qualifying fourth, and

*(opposite)* **Chassis 8612-03 active suspension car during a test at Mid-Ohio in 1987.**

# The Racers

The speed, power, braking, and cornering abilities of the GTP cars evolved from the flat-bottom cars of the 1960s and '70s, for example the Porsche 917K, to become ultra-sophisticated machines capable of significantly lower lap times on the same tracks. Tire technology improved dramatically, and with electronic management of engines, fuel, and suspensions, the GTP cars became highly refined machines that established a new generation of racers—better, faster, and quicker than ever before.

The GTPs were the cars that the world's best road racing drivers wanted to drive. IMSA set the format that produced the finest prototype racing seen anywhere, including the similar European World Endurance Championship series for Group C cars that went through all sorts of convulsions. In contrast, IMSA GTP was stable and grew each year, as did the number of fans, the race winnings, the number of sponsors, and the end-of-year jackpot awarded to the champion. In terms of the number of factory entries, the quality of independent teams, and the level of competition, the 1981, 1986, and 1988 years stand out as exceptional.

While the cost of racing steadily climbed, media attention attracted a worldwide audience that produced superstars. Meanwhile, behind-the-scenes maneuvering and self-serving politics were ever-present. In addition to rapidly advancing technology during this period, a steady diet of rule changes continually fed the complex entanglement involving everyone associated with the sport. If any team perceived that a rule change favored their competitors, protests were loud and long. While rule changes continually favored less costly ways to race, namely stock-block engines, the series in the mid-'80s was, for the most part, dominated by Porsche, whose teams tended to win races regardless of rule changes and advances made by competitors.

The large number of Porsches in IMSA GTP racing virtually ensured high finishes in every race, and Al Holbert's 962s won more races than any other team. Although the Porsche factory was not directly involved, appearances to the fans were just the opposite. Porsche's successes were, however, largely due to Holbert, who was GTP champion in 1983, '85, and '86. During his GTP years, he was also team driver in three wins at Le Mans (1983, '86, and '87). He was IMSA's first million dollar winner. Unfortunately, he was killed in a private plane crash on September 30, 1988, ending a brilliant career. GTP racing and its fans lost a true gentleman of the sport, a driver and team owner who helped shape the professionalism of the series. His competitors lost a great adversary as well.

GTP racing's top drivers, Brian Redman, Al Holbert, Derek Bell, Sarel Van Der Merwe, Geoff Brabham, and several others were an overwhelming presence that shaped the sport. They were the visible figures of very effective racing teams who wrote the records that made the drivers great, even legendary. Redman revolutionized GTP racing with the Cooke-Woods

*(opposite)* **The short tail Corvette GTP (HU-8610/02) with dual wing, showing the final form of the car as raced.**

Lola T-600 of 1981. Van Der Merwe and the GM Goodwrench GTP Corvette were stunning record setters in 1986. Holbert's team dominated the series in 1985 and '86 with methodical attention to details. Britain's Tom Walkinshaw Racing Jaguars came in 1988 and created enormous interest in the series, while Bob Tullius's Group 44 Jaguars gave the series lessons in stock-block prototype racing. Then came Brabham in the sensational Electramotive Nissan ZX-Turbo cars—winners four years running. A host of independents racing all sorts of cars gave the series extraordinary diversity. IMSA GTP was great racing with great machines and great drivers.

The story of Doc Bundy's rise to GTP's top shelf offers insight into this great American series of racing, and illustrates how it influenced a generation of racing drivers.

Bundy started out in go-carts at about age twelve and honed his killer instinct for six years. He really wanted to road race, but having grown up in a small community in Ohio coal country, he did not know how to get into it. Indy car racing was his biggest thrill, but he got drafted into the service and spent two years in the army in Vietnam. In 1970, he met some guys who were into sports car racing, and while he was in Vietnam, he ordered a Corvette. It wasn't delivered until a couple of months after he got back to the United States.

At the time, he was working at the Canton, Ohio, airport and met some friends who also had Corvettes. They went to see a Can-Am race at Mid-Ohio, his first race, and he was hooked. He followed the Can-Am for the next couple of years, paying special attention to Formula 5000 and the racing skills of Brian Redman. That's what he wanted to do, but

A

**A. Elliot Forbes-Robinson set a Sebring track record pole, the fastest race lap, another track record, and with Al Holbert led the race for ten hours, then lost on a pit stop to change a failed turbo. Robinson went on to win the IMSA Championship. Sarel Van Der Merwe in the Hendrick Corvette GTP cars finished the season a distant tenth.**

**B. Tom Walkinshaw Racing fielded 6.0-liter Jaguar GTP cars and won the marque's first 24-Hours victory in thirty years at Daytona in 1988.**

B

since he had no money, all his friends laughed when he said he wanted to race.

Bundy was determined to get into racing, so he quit his job and went to Florida, where he convinced Peter Gregg to hire him as a gofer. Gregg was IMSA's top driver and raced most of his highly successful career driving for Brumos Porsche, his own dealership, located in Jacksonville. Bundy went to all the races with Gregg's team, but it wasn't until May or June that Gregg officially hired him. Eventually, he convinced Gregg to keep him on and got his first salary, not much—about $90 a week—still as a gofer. To keep his expenses down, Bundy set up home in a corner of the shop.

After a time, he became sort of an apprentice mechanic, but that wasn't what he wanted to do; he wanted to be a driver. Gregg told him: "Doc, nobody is going to give you a $50,000 car to drive." Bundy was twenty-three or so, and if anyone told him "no" to anything, he was inspired even more.

He spent two seasons with Gregg, and he learned a lot about what it took to win, because Gregg won—lots of races. Bundy says he learned the mental approach to racing from Gregg. He said, "Peter was a genius; he would psyche his opponents with the little things he did."

Toward the end of Bundy's first year with Gregg, Al Holbert got one of the new 3-liter Porsche racing engines. Gregg wanted one, so he bought it from Holbert and sent Bundy to Pennsylvania to pick it up. Arriving on a Friday, Bundy was going to start right back to Jacksonville when Holbert asked if he would like to stick around for the weekend. That invitation became an opportunity. After contacting Gregg, who agreed that it was okay for Bundy to stay over, Bundy stayed at Holbert's house, where they talked racing the entire weekend. Toward the end of the weekend, Holbert told Bundy that he would like for him to join his racing team. That's when Bundy revealed that he really wanted to drive, and since he and Holbert were about the same age, there would be little opportunity to drive, because there was only room for one driver.

Bundy went back to Brumos, but maintained his contact with Holbert. About six months into his second year with Gregg, he decided to leave Gregg's team at year's end and did so on amiable terms.

During that time, Gregg and Holbert teamed for a race or two, Holbert with Gregg in Gregg's car, and Gregg with Holbert in Holbert's car. Bundy crewed for Gregg when they raced Holbert's car. By direct comparison, he saw the difference in the cars and realized that Holbert was much more of an engineer than Gregg, a realization that hinted at how much more he could learn about cars on the Holbert team. He had to make a decision.

A trucking firm in Jacksonville put together a tube frame Monza at the end of 1974 and offered Bundy the job of driving if he would be crew chief as well. He did not believe himself to be crew chief material, so he decided to go with Holbert and remained with the team for the next five years. During this time, he orchestrated Holbert's move to the Chevrolet Monza.

Bundy recognized that IMSA favored that type of car, and everyone on the Monza team knew that their stiffest competition, the guy they would always have to beat, was Peter Gregg, who was newly installed in a well-supported BMW program. Bundy took it upon himself to tell the Dekon team that if they were ever going to win with the Monza they needed Al Holbert.

Dekon was the factory operation for Chevrolet. When everyone involved, including Al Holbert, got together with Vince Piggins at Chevrolet and worked out a deal, it was a winner. Holbert won the championship in 1976.

Because of the ties to Dekon and connection with Lee Dysktra, who designed the cars, association with Chevrolet progressed from there, and Holbert decided that he wanted to try stock cars. Bundy was bitterly opposed to the move because it was a radical departure that he believed would put them off the IMSA track for two years. Then, Holbert had a pretty bad crash at Pocono in his Monte Carlo. As the car burned, Holbert realized that on the limited schedule he was racing, he wasn't going to be successful.

Meanwhile, Can-Am was coming back together, and Bundy read that Carl Hogan was putting together a team. He wrote Hogan, once again promoting Al Holbert, while hoping that he would get to do some road racing. Bundy and Holbert flew out to St. Louis to meet with Hogan and to look at the car. A deal was quickly put together, and they were Can-Am racing.

Dykstra was brought back into the fold with the Lola that Hogan was running. The popular Formula 5000 chassis at the time was the Lola T-332. For the Can-Am, the cars were converted from open wheel to full body cars. Using that experience, the team designed and built their own Can-Am car. That was in the era of skirts and ground effects. It was originally a Busch car, then it became a CRC Chemicals car, red and white. Having had a hand in the car from the very beginning, Bundy really wanted to drive it.

The car was built at Holbert's shop, designed by Lee Dykstra, and thought to have been designated the HR-1 (Holbert Racing-1). The engine was based on the production Chevrolet small-block engine. Then, in 1979, Bundy got the break that began his driving career: Holbert helped him get a job racing Porsche 924s in SCCA national competition.

Bundy's career progressed to the 924 Turbo version in Trans-Am racing in 1981, and he ran the full 1982 season in the car. That year brought huge success. BFGoodrich was promoting their tires and put together a deal that took him to the 24-Hours of Le Mans. He teamed up with Jim Busby and they won the IMSA GT category with the car (2,307.88 miles at 96.16 MPH) and finished sixteenth overall, a stunning achievement for a first effort at Le Mans.

Bundy believes that his success with Porsches and his association with Al Holbert made things happen. He and Holbert, along with Rick Mears, drove a twenty-four-hour race in the 924, and he had some drives in 935 Porsches and a March-Chevy GTP—the car that Holbert had won Miami with—and he drove the Aston Martin Nimrod prototype.

# DOC BUNDY

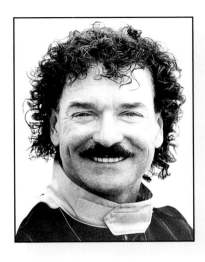

**"I had been with some impressive teams, but I had never been with a team that had that much talent. Everyone on that team was like a surgeon in ability."**

➤ I had done one-off races here and there in GT racing with the Porsche 930, the Monza once—scary cars—so I had some track time. Then Al [Holbert] asked me to do a proposal to Porsche for racing the 924. So, I made a proposal, from grass roots on up, and Al submitted it. Porsche wanted to get the 924's reputation up, so they wanted the cars to run in SCCA national competition. They picked Al as the development team, and he picked me as the driver. Of course, they didn't want me. They wanted someone like Al or Hurley Haywood. Al didn't want to do club racing, and he convinced them that they could get me for nothing. What he was really doing was trying to give me my break, and to get me off his back for driving his cars.

We got a car from the factory, and I began driving the Porsche 924 in D-Production, but it wasn't very good. We worked on it, worked on it, worked on it, then we built a car of our own in 1980. It was a great car. Dykstra did the design. Then we decided that since I would be driving this car, I couldn't work for Al any more. The next day,

Road Atlanta called and asked if I wanted to be instructor for road racing. I had always wanted to live in the Gainesville area, so I moved to Georgia to be the track driving instructor and kept on racing the 924.

Nobody had won with the 924 yet, so it was a race to see who would get the first win. We entered our first race at Bryar, New Hampshire. It was a national race, and we qualified second without much of a chance of winning. I got the jump at the start and led into the first turn, then several cars went by me and were gone. About halfway through the race, my guys hung out the pit board with P1 on it. That went on for the last six or seven laps, and I was wondering what they wanted me to pit for. The car was running great. That's not what it meant. [It meant Position 1.] I took the checkered flag and came into the pit where my guys were all jumping around. We had won our first time out! If I remember right, we were in twelve events that year and we won ten, including the National Championship here at Road Atlanta.

*(opposite)* **IMSA GTP racing in the early 1980s drew the finest of world class competition. Some entrants, like this Aston Martin Nimrod introduced in 1983, were unsuccessful against the March chassis cars powered by Chevrolet or Porsche engines.**

win the race. Reliability was getting better, but we had engine problems, and Ryan had to sort those things out as this project went along. A lot of our testing was done at races, in races, and that was somewhat disconcerting. But we had developed such a close-knit group that testing was always a lot of fun. Normally we would gain. Some of the oddest things would make us go faster.

Once at IRP [Indianapolis Raceway Park] we were using the Indy cars as our measuring point, and I got going faster than Eddie Cheever. We didn't find a tremendous change in the car that made us gain two seconds a lap; we started letting air pressure out of the tires. Suddenly, that car hooked up. We tried letting out two more PSI and two more and at the end of the test we were scratching our heads because every time we let air out of the tires, the car would go faster. We knew how dangerous it was because we could pop the tire off the rim if the air pressure got too low. There are some high speed turns at IRP, especially that first turn. We're cranking 180, 190 miles per hour down the straightaway into the first turn, a fourth-gear turn, so we go in at well over one hundred miles per hour. That's cooking, and to trust that the tires are going to stay on the rims is rather nerve-racking. Of course the Good-year guys just about shot us. They were absolutely against it; we had to sneak letting air out of the tires at races. At some tracks it worked, at some it didn't. If we dropped air pressure one pound, they would really be unhappy with us.

There were things like this that went on all the time. I had been bugging the team, bugging and bugging them about shocks, because I knew that the Indy cars were going through the shock thing at that time, and I had heard that they were finding tremendous gains. That all started with the Fox shock, then Penske hired the guy away from Fox and the shocks became Penske shocks, the same thing, really. Finally I convinced the team to get a set for us, so they did. We had two cars at a test session at Mid-Ohio, and we put them on the second car. Sarel went out in the car first and came back in all excited saying, "Get in, Doc! Get in. Get in." I wanted to know what he was excited

about, but he wouldn't tell me. I went out for about three laps and came back in, and I didn't want to get out because it was so much fun. I opened the door, and everyone was smiling. I said, "It has suspension!"

Up to that time, if you touched a curb at any racetrack, you were history. You hit a curb and you're next trying to gather the car up to keep from crashing, or you spin, or crash. It was a difficult car to drive, before the shocks, and I don't remember exactly when those shocks went on, halfway through the first year, '86, or into the second year, but when it happened, it was like a new car.

Before installing those shocks, we would make changes to the car and it really didn't make much of a difference. When we put the shocks on the car, we could make a subtle change, and the car would feel it. Finally, we had a car under us, so we really started progressing. About that same time, the Lotus active suspension stuff was going on, but Chevrolet didn't want to spend any money on the car.

I didn't know what the big project was when they brought the Lotus engineers in, but I knew that Lotus knew suspensions. So, I thought, I was finally going to get a car with a real suspension. At one point—they were so secretive—I said something to Peter Wright, the head of the active suspension work at Lotus, "So, you are finally going to design me a front suspension?" He just smiled and didn't tell me anything. That's the way that era went.

We knew the car was on the heavy side, but we had some good successes anyway, especially at Road Atlanta. We won that race, of all things, because the Al Holbert car couldn't get grip. That had always been our problem, but for some reason we hit the right combination that weekend. We had tested a fair bit, and I knew the track, but there was a whole series of things that happened that should have prevented us from winning that race. I was one of the reasons not to win it.

Sarel had hurt his neck and was spending limited time in the car, so I was doing the bulk of the setup. He got in to qualify it and got out. The team guys were concerned about what we were going to do. For Sunday morning warm-up, they told me to do

all the warm-up, to scrub tires, bed brake pads, and so forth, to check out the car.

I had been riding my motorcycle all week, and on my way to the track, I went off the road big! I live close to the track, and it happened about two miles from my house. I got the bike up and took it home. I had skid marks and my clothes were torn, so I took off my leather jacket, changed my pants, and cleaned up. I got in my car and drove into the track about one minute from starting warm-up. When I got to the trailer, they were complaining, "Where have you been? The car's running...." So, I ran in the trailer to change, in a lot of pain, and Ken Howes came in to chew on me a little more. He took one look at me and said, "You crashed that motorcycle! Oh, my God. Sarel's hurt, now you're hurt. Oh, my God."

Ken is the king of worry. I used to love putting him on all the time. The guy could worry a tree down. I told him, "Ken, you're not going to say anything to anybody. I'll be fine." He didn't buy it. "You can't drive. Look at you! Look at your back. Oh, my God, what are we going to do?" I told him, "I can drive the car, and you're not telling anybody." He paced and paced in the trailer.

I go out for morning warm-up and did OK. I told him everything was all right. "Yeah, right," he complained. "You can't drive; Sarel can't drive. What are we going to do?"

Sarel started the race, and we were doing really good, leading when we came to the first pit stop when I got in. By then I was stiffening up, but I was so excited; the car was good. We were smack on with the car, but when I came back in, I was hurting. Sarel went back out, but soon called in that he couldn't drive. I would have to finish the race. Now, everyone was worried. We had cut the window to the end of the race as close as we could, so I get back in. Now we're racing with John Paul for the one time that the March-Buick was working. He had broken every time, but not this race. John and I are racing. He is faster than me at certain points on the track, and he outhandled me at others, but I am faster on the high speed sections of track.

Knowing Road Atlanta the way I do, I knew the tactics I would have to play to take advantage of my capabilities over his strengths, so I had to pass him on the straight and be ahead of him in the turns to Turn 7. If I was leading through Seven, I could get off better, and he could not get me down the straight. It was back and forth, back and forth through traffic. I'd get blocked, and he'd get by. Then I'd get back by him down the straight. We had a great GTP race going, one of the better races that year. Everyone in the pits was thinking "fuel," and I was talking back and forth with them on the radio while trying to hold back on the RPM, because that's the only way to save fuel, to short shift. I was holding back when I could, and running the car when I had to. With one or two laps to go, we came under the bridge into Twelve, I was leading, and I saw John peel off into pit lane. He had to come in for fuel. Well, we had it then.

John is a good friend, and I had seen that team struggle all season. So, it was with mixed emotions that I was glad we won. They had struggled for so long, and they had a pretty good car. But, we had won. Few people knew of our troubles, though, Sarel with his neck problem and me skinned from head to toe.

The other race we won that year was later at West Palm, a street race. It was a mess, the site of one of our best victories and our greatest losses the next year when our best car burned.

In that particular race we were hooked up pretty good, and I was having a battle with Darin Brassfield in the BFGoodrich 962 Porsche. We were battling back and forth in the late stages of the race when there was a caution. They restarted with one lap to go, and Darin was trying to un-lap himself by muscling his way through the turns and knocked me wide, but didn't get through. That let Brian Redman through in the Jaguar. But what none of us knew, and I didn't know at the time, was that Brian was in the lead. This all happened with one corner to go! Then we go up a little chute to the last corner, an absolutely dead-stop turn back to the last straightaway and the flag.

Prior to the caution, when I went by the pits, Ryan had heard the engine and said it was going flat. They called me on the radio, and I told them, "Yeah, it's gone flat." They got all excited and said it was the alternator and got back on the radio, telling me to cut off all the electrics. West Palm is really hot, and that meant that I had to turn off the cool suit. I said, "No!"

Then we were under caution, and they told me to turn everything off. I kept saying, "No, no. Do you know how hot it is in here?" Then they started telling me over the radio all the things they were going to do for me if I would just cut the cool suit off. I should have gotten all of it in writing; I'd be a rich man if I had. They were convinced that the car was not going to make it. I already knew why they were hearing the sounds they were; I did a major, major miss-shift, over-revved it big time! I was certain that all the pushrods were bent, and the valves, too.

So now we're on the last lap, and Brian got by into the last turn. This turn was so tight that you couldn't make it unless you went from the far outside to the inside around it. Brian went in and tried to make the classic line, but I stayed into it so deep that I just got inside of him into the turn. I forced my car inside knowing that if I didn't, Darin would. He was right on me. I went in too deep, locked up the brakes, and couldn't make the turn. Brian turns to make the corner and knocks the nose of my car into the corner. Darin hits me in the back end, turning me in the right direction, and I'm looking straight down the straightaway to the finish line. I put it in first gear and floor it. At this point, the last corner, I didn't care about the tires, even if I burned them off. Well, I figured, with the car spinning, swinging back and forth, it would be hard for someone to pass me. So, I burned them. I took the checkered flag just barely ahead of Darin. The car sounded like it was going to explode. The engine was literally junk.

We had won, and the guys in the pits were talking to me on the radio. I asked, "Can I turn my cool suit on?" I thought I was about to die it was so hot.

Riding around under caution, it was unbelievably hot. I put a thermometer in the cockpit once, and it showed 140 degrees. I didn't ever want to see a thermometer again. When you're wearing all that cool suit stuff, with it not working, it's even hotter.

After the race when we were back at the hotel, everyone was there. Sarel and Ken always took great glee in getting people intoxicated, but I'm not much of a drinker, having chosen to move away from the stuff when I started racing. But every once in a while I would have a few drinks, and Sarel lived for those times because he claimed I was the funniest man alive after I had a few. Well, they got equal pleasure in getting a few drinks in Ryan, but the only thing we could get him on was a specific wine he liked. Even then, he didn't drink very much. Well, he got to going on about how good I did, and I asked if I was finally okay with him. He said, "Yes, you're okay with me."

Well, now I had him where I wanted him and asked, "Ryan, will you do me one little favor, and I'll never ask for another one?"

"I'll do whatever you want," he said. "What's the favor you want? You want more horsepower, you got it, Doc."

I said, "No, when you get this engine back home, will you just dump it in the trash can?"

Well, he was surprised. I told him that when he took the heads off, he was going to dump everything out anyway. It was totally destroyed! I told him, "I missed a shift so big, I didn't think the car would finish the race."

"Oh, that's OK," he said. "You won the race."

About a week later, I got a call from Ryan. He was sober. He told me, "Doc, you were right. I took the heads off and dumped it all out. There wasn't anything worth saving."

That was some of the good times. There were lots of them. This was a close-knit group with a lot of friendship. When we went to two cars and I had my own, Sarel would concentrate on qualifying, and I concentrated on race setup. A lot of the time, he wanted to qualify in my car and would actually go faster than in his car. He liked for me to do race setup, and that was why he was upset when they decided not to renew my contract at the end of '87. It was not a team decision, as it turned out; it was done in a way that messed me up for quite a while. In fact, I was ready to quit racing altogether. All that fall, they had been telling me that my contract was going to be renewed. Then I had a bad crash at Del Mar. Sarel had gone out early; he spun right in front of me. He got the rear tires spinning, then the car got sideways and hit the wall. It knocked him across into the other wall. When you hit a wall at a street circuit, you usually get both of them. I was in pretty good shape and was looking for a top-three for sure, and maybe a shot at winning. On a restart along a high-speed kink on the back of the track, my car just didn't turn. I contended that I had a flat tire, but my crew chief looked at it and told me the tire was not cut. The car just didn't turn.

I was lucky. To this day, I have a scar on the back of my legs because an A-arm went between my legs. It could easily have been much worse. That would have been the end of it for me. The Chevrolet people were very strange that weekend, and I think that was the excuse they wanted to get me out of the project. I never publicly said the car was "dog shit," Sarel's favorite term. I was more diplomatic about it. But to the engineers, I was hard on their case. I will not give up. If I want something for my car to make it a winner, I want it, and I will not give the team a moment's peace until I get it, because it's the car that gives the wins. I always wanted to make the car better. All along, we gave up some little things that would have added up to be worthwhile—downforce on the front end because of the Corvette shape, overweight, mechanically we gave up some advantages. The Chevrolet people would always come back saying they couldn't change the nose because it would not look like a Corvette. I argued that it didn't look like a Corvette anyway, it just had the name. Maybe it could be described as a future Corvette; just make the changes to improve the car.

So, there was always a difference of opinion, and I later found out that anything that happened over a weekend of racing, my name was getting put on the reports back to GM. They were building a case to get me out, that's what it was all about. I didn't know that, and it had nothing to do with the team. I had simply pissed off the engineers, and Chevrolet decided to reduce its involvement in the project.

All through my driving, I raced the 6-cylinder cars. We talked about the V8, and Sarel got on the bandwagon big time, but I wasn't convinced that the V8 would make the car better. I talked to Ryan about it and left the engines up to him, but I felt that the problems we had were related more to the engine management system than the engines themselves. The Chevrolet engine guy would come in and change a chip just before a race, and it would ruin the car. At Sears Point, for instance, we had the car hooked up pretty good, and I was looking for a good finish, then he changed the chip. I had nothing but problems, and eventually the engine broke itself, even though I was trying to save it by trying to finish. Right when I was running, the engine would just change, timing, fuel mixtures, and so on.

At that time, I maintained that Nissan was the coming competition because they started with the same chassis we had, the Lola 710, and stayed with the 6-cylinder. They set about curing all the problems they had, and in '87 their cars could simply pull away from ours because they could put the power down. We couldn't. I campaigned that we needed to address the problems with our cars, but everyone was talking V8. I kept saying that Nissan was not going to the V8; we had to do to our cars what it took to accept the power that Ryan could give us. Power wasn't the problem, getting it to the track surface was the problem, and he was not going to be able to give us the power from a V8.

Maybe my opinions had something to do with my departure. I thought we needed a chassis and suspension engineer to work specifically with us, but we didn't have one. The Nissan engineer made their cars better and better.

The greatest sadness I had in the program was at West Palm in '87 when we lost a car, our best car. It was a new car, just its second or third race, and it was so much better than the earlier car. It had the tub that the team had completely built themselves. They took all their knowledge to that point and built the lightest, strongest, least flexible car we had. I could feel that it was a better car, though not completely worked out yet, but it was going to be a winner. Then the fuel tank pressurized and expanded into the engine pulley that drilled into the tank. Fuel poured down into the undertray, and the turbos lit the fuel. The fire crew took forever to get there, and even though I tried to do something by grabbing a fire extinguisher from the corner workers, it wrote off our best car. IMSA was reluctant to put the safety car out, and the "Keystone firemen" took several laps to get there. It was a monumental error.

Seven days before I was to begin testing for the '88 season, I was on the phone with Ken talking about where and when we would be testing. Less than thirty minutes later, I got another call. I was up, talking about how we were going to get it right this year when I was told, "Doc, this isn't easy. I'm sorry, your contract is not renewed."

I wanted to know what happened. He told me that someday I would learn the truth, but the people I might think were the cause were not. Later I learned that it was not the team or the team ownership, and those were the important things to me. The only explanation I got from Chevrolet was that Herb Fischel thought I did not fit. Years before, we had gotten the short end of the stick on the Dekon Monza program when I was with Al Holbert, and I knew then how dangerous the politics at Chevrolet could be.

Overall, from the racing standpoint, I was ready to quit. There were no rides that late, all the contracts had been done, so nothing was available. The way they did it put a question mark in everyone's mind; is there something wrong with Doc Bundy?

Then, Tommy Morrison from Albany, Georgia, convinced me to drive an Escort Race in Camaros. I was reluctant, but I did it, and I've never had so much fun. Then I did the Corvette Challenge one year, which I refused to do again because they picked who would win. If you got the right chip, you could win. If they didn't like you, you didn't get the right chip. All year long, my car would run great for about ten laps, then the temperatures would all go up, the car would lose power and slow down. In the final race, to try to win me back for the next season, they gave me the right chip.

The car never lost power, never ran hot, and that really made me mad. "That's it," I said. "I'm definitely not doing this any more." I ran the full season with Tommy and won a couple of races. We were undefeated that year, usually finishing one-two. My teammate won the championship. The cars were good, and I had a ball. Then I put the Lotus program together for '89, and raced with Tommy in the ZR-1 Corvettes. Those cars were getting better and better. I still think the engine in that car is the neatest V8 I've ever driven. It is so flexible and has so much potential.

Well, that's it; the story of my racing the GTP Corvette and more. ➤

Bobby Rahal leads the James Weaver/Price Cobb Porsche 962 to finish fifth overall in the final race of chassis number HU-8610/02 as a 6.0-liter V8 car.

B

A

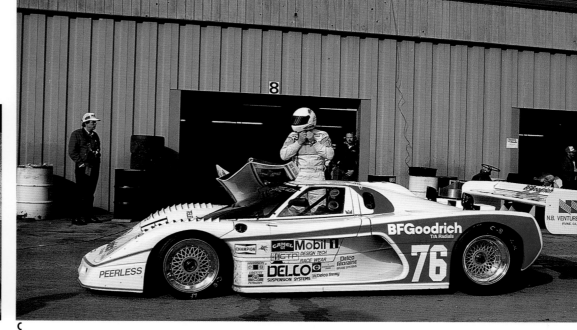

C

and Watkins Glen—they closed out the Corvette GTP legacy at the Glen. The last race for a Corvette GTP was on July 2, 1989. The car qualified tenth, and departed with just eleven laps completed.

Like the Hendrick active suspension car of 1987, the Peerless Corvette GTP ventured into computer-controlled equipment. The car was fitted with an active braking system from GM's Delco division. The system was essentially updated anti-lock braking similar to the production Corvette.

At that point, the competitive life of the Corvette GTP had expired, and the cars were retired as both factory and private entries.

Peerless Automotive Engineering and its racing team were headed by Bob Carson, whose insight into his team illuminates the Corvette GTP saga.

On December 23, 1987, Carson placed an order to Carl Haas Automobile Imports in Chicago for one of the latest Lola chassis cars. John Pierce at Chevrolet was also involved in initially providing contacts and recommendations. The car cost $202,500 FOB Chicago and required a $50,000 down payment with the purchase order. Delivery to Peerless was targeted for March 15. Later, an additional tub and spares were ordered as well. The tub cost $42,000. The costs of the engine, testing, development, and racing added to the exercise and illustrate the enormous costs associated with GTP racing.

IMSA records show that the fourth-place finish at Columbus earned $8,500 for the Peerless team. At the Del Mar Fairgrounds that year, the Budweiser-sponsored car was not running after seventy laps and earned $2,000. Initially running well at Tampa, the tenth overall finish, while not running, brought in $8,000. In the first round of the '89 season held at West Palm Beach, the car was not running after forty-four laps and once again secured just $2,000. At Mid-Ohio in June, an engine failure sidelined the car after twenty-seven laps. Earnings were $4,000. At Watkins Glen, not running after eighty-one laps netted $3,000. Total earnings of $27,500 for the Peerless Racing team illustrate the disproportionate reward for participating in such a costly sport. Only those teams that consistently finished high and won some races earned substantially from the sport. For example, at the Glen,

the winning Electramotive Nissan ZX-Turbo (Geoff Brabham and Chip Robinson) took home $77,000. The second-place finisher got just $20,000.

When major corporate sponsorships came into IMSA GTP racing, for instance R.J. Reynolds as sponsor for the Camel GT series in the early 1970s, costs escalated. Were it not for advertising and promotion funds through sponsorships, both major and minor, the sport would not have attracted the world class attention it did. Having grown from initial concept in 1969 to a leading series of racing in a little over ten years, IMSA racing was a spotlight sport and its winning teams enjoyed great media attention and promotion that made drivers into superstars. Financial reward for drivers typically came from purses and whatever income they received from driving and sponsors. Teams received financial support from their sponsors, and major sponsors such as Budweiser poured vast amounts of money into advertising. A top team enjoyed success measured in many ways, and fans got great racing, but a mid-running team or a back marker who was there because the guys loved to race had difficulty surviving. When a major sponsor withdrew, the team had to scramble to find financing or get out.

While the 1989 GTP season will be remembered for the diversity of foreign entrants—Nissan, Toyota, Jaguar, and Porsche—along with the Nissan and Jaguar duels and Nissan victories, American entries were few and not very successful. Except for the Bob Earl/Jim Miller second-place finish in the GTE World Challenge in the Spice-Chevrolet, and Wayne Taylor's pole position at Del Mar in the Spice-Pontiac, the American influence in GTP racing that year was minimal. While American engines in the hands of private racing teams had a presence, the factories did not, and lack of sufficient funding severely limited the prospects against the much better supported teams.

The Peerless Corvette GTP team did not race again after Watkins Glen, and the car was sold in December 1989 for $178,000. Everyone involved went on to other things, and the new owners had an exciting and beautiful car that was part of IMSA's spectacular era of GTP racing.

**A. Jacques Villeneuve (left) and Scott Goodyear (right) were Peerless team drivers in 1989.**

**B. Road Atlanta shortly before Jack Baldwin's flip.**

**C. Suiting up for a test session at Road Atlanta in 1989, the Peerless Corvette GTP is now a short tail car.**

Atlanta before we entered the car in its first event. That first event was the Columbus, Ohio, GTP race, which was on the second of October, the first outing for the car, and we finished fourth. That was a pretty good showing for the first time out. We had acquired the Budweiser sponsorship for the balance of the year, and the car was known as the Bud GTP Corvette. Baldwin and Hobbs were the test drivers as well as race drivers. Will Moody was the crew chief and Brad Francis was team manager. Chevrolet race shop engineers worked with us, and we had close involvement with John Pierce, Dick Amacher, and Dan Engel.

Then we moved on to the GTP race in Del Mar, California. Our run there was not very good. We had problems with getting power down. The track had just been resurfaced and the sealer on it was extremely slick. We had so much torque that the car was slipping and sliding all over the track. In the race, we moved up on the first lap, then another car hit us in the rear end, tearing one of our side pods off. So we had to pit to make some quick repairs, then went back out about two laps down and ran several more laps before we had another shunt. We finally retired the car.

After we repaired the car, we moved on to the final race of the year, the Tampa GTP race, and did well. Jack Baldwin drove the car in the beginning of the race and David Hobbs was co-driving. David had been with us driving in the previous races as well. Jack moved up as high as second overall, then diced back and forth between second and third, then made an excellent pit stop and changed drivers. Hobbs went back out in fourth place and was working his way up to third when he came together with Pete Halsmer in one of the Ford Probes. Hobbs spun into one of the tire barriers, which retired the car. That was a big disappointment because we were looking for a high finish in that race.

In the three races we were in, two were pretty sound. We had one good, high finish and another for sure if we had not had the shunt. So, overall, things looked good for the full 1989 season, which we planned to run.

In the off-season, we made some additional modifications to the car. We built our own molds for the nose and fabricated our own nose piece, and into the second event, we shortened the pods to produce the short tail version, similar to what Hendrick had done with his cars. We built our own pods, our own shortened tail, and our own center-mount wing, then proceeded to take that car to Road Atlanta. Early on we had some problems, and Jack got upside down in the car.

In testing, the car proved to be very unstable. We put the old nose back on, and ran a few laps to build some stability back into the car. When Jack got on the brakes at one point, it got away from him and got on the fence where it did a slow roll. That was in Turn 3. No other cars were involved. Well, we put the car on the trailer and brought it home. We didn't even get in that event.

At that point, Jack was leery of the car, and the other driver we had, Tom Pumpelly, was also concerned with the car, so we made a team decision at that time to put two new drivers in the car to sort it out, hoping to make it competitive. We got Scott Goodyear and Jacques Villeneuve in the car to finish out the season.

The first event after that was West Palm, where we did fairly well. We moved up into the top ten, although we had not qualified that well. We had sorted out some of the problems and had moved up to sixth when the engine quit on us. So we retired. That was indicative of things to come. We ended up spending our season on motor problems. We had done some development work with David Billes of Performance Engineering, who had supplied all the engines for the previous year. They had proven to be good, durable units, but when we did some redesign on heads and pistons, trying to extract more horsepower and to up our torque curve, we got into a situation that valve size became a limiting factor, and we lost dependability and reliability of our engines.

We skipped the next race, Lime Rock, then ran Mid-Ohio. At that race, we thought maybe things were coming back our way. We qualified fourth or fifth overall in GTP, but in the race, the motor grem-

(opposite) One of the beautiful GTP cars as raced at Del Mar, 1988. The Peerless Corvette GTP ran its last race at Watkins Glen, July 2, 1989.

than Hendrick was getting with his V8 cars. We were generating 680 to 690 horsepower on the

C. Peerless Racing team engineer Terry Satchell (right) and electronics technician Rae William (center) chat with a friend.

## CHASSIS: HU-8610/01    *(continued)*

| Event | Date | Car Number | Driver(s) | Qualifying Position | Qualifying Time (Pole) | Finish | Laps Completed | Race Comments |
|-------|------|-----------|-----------|---------------------|------------------------|--------|----------------|---------------|
| Mid-Ohio | 6/7/87 | 52 | Sarel Van Der Merwe<br>Doc Bundy | 5 | —<br>(1:19.865) | 3 | 125 of 129 | |
| West Palm Beach | 6/21/87 | 52 | Sarel Van Der Merwe<br>Doc Bundy | 1 | 1:05.130<br>Record | 18NR | 51 of 148 | Led 16 laps. Van Der Merwe set fastest race lap, a track record of 1:05.960. Car burned. |
| Portland | 7/26/87 | 52 | Doc Bundy | 4 | 0:59.621<br>(0:57.778) | 7 | 94 of 97 | Car rebuilt with original tub. |
| Sears Point | 8/2/87 | 52 | Sarel Van Der Merwe<br>Doc Bundy | 5 | —<br>(1:25.624) | 3 | 75 of 75 | |
| San Antonio | 9/6/87 | 22 | Sarel Van Der Merwe<br>Doc Bundy | 1 | 1:07.855<br>Record | 3 | 141 of 142 | |
| Del Mar | 10/25/87 | 52 | Doc Bundy | 7 | 1:06.692<br>(1:03.849) | 22NR | 18 of 97 | Crashed. |

**CHASSIS: HU-8610/02**   **Delivered: June 20, 1986**   **Entrant: Hendrick Motorsports**
**Engine: 1986: 3.4-liter (209 CID) Turbo-V6; 1987: 3.0-liter (183 CID) Turbo-V6; 1988: 6.0-liter (366 CID) V8**

| Event | Date | Car Number | Driver(s) | Qualifying Position | Qualifying Time (Pole) | Finish | Laps Completed | Race Comments |
|---|---|---|---|---|---|---|---|---|
| Daytona Finale | 10/26/86 | 22 | Doc Bundy | 17 | 1:43.654 (1:39.564) | 50NR | 17 of 97 | |
| Miami | 3/1/87 | 22 | Sarel Van Der Merwe Doc Bundy | 3 | 1:12.874 (1:09.634) | 21NR | 103 of 133 | |
| Mid-Ohio | 6/7/87 | 22 | Michael Andretti John Andretti | 3 | — (1:19.865) | 11 | 114 of 129 | |
| Watkins Glen | 7/5/87 | 52 | Sarel Van Der Merwe Doc Bundy | 3 | — (1:00.704) | 23NR | 37 of 128 | Led 24 laps. Set track straightaway speed trap record of 205.7 MPH. |
| Portland | 7/26/87 | 22 | Sarel Van Der Merwe | 3 | 0:59.576 (0:57.778) | 4 | 96 of 97 | |
| Road America | 8/16/87 | 52 | Sarel Van Der Merwe Doc Bundy | 2 | — (2:02.745) | 39NR | 58 of 81 | |
| Del Mar | 10/25/87 | 22 | Sarel Van Der Merwe | 6 | 1:05.144 (1:03.849) | 26NR | 1 of 97 | |
| Miami | 2/28/88 | 22 | Elliott Forbes-Robinson David Hobbs | 10 | 1:13.940 (1:09.802) | 23 | 77 of 124 | |
| Sebring | 3/20/88 | 22 | Sarel Van Der Merwe Elliott Forbes-Robinson | 6 | 1:58.861 (1:55.856) | 43NR | 151 of 318 | |
| Road Atlanta | 4/10/88 | 22 | Elliott Forbes-Robinson Didier Theys | 4 | 1:13.405 (1:11.596) | 8 | 117 of 124 | Fitted with new tub. |
| West Palm Beach | 4/24/88 | 22 | Sarel Van Der Merwe Arie Luyendyk | 8 | — (0:58.762) | 28NR | 6 of 149 | |
| Lime Rock | 5/30/88 | 52 | Sarel Van Der Merwe Elliott Forbes-Robinson | 5 | 0:46.336 (0:44.885) | 7 | 144 of 150 | |
| Mid-Ohio | 6/5/88 | 52 | Elliott Forbes-Robinson Wally Dallenbach, Jr. | 10 | 1:23.800 (1:19.995) | 7 | 126 of 129 | First Hendrick Motorsports car to be fitted with V8 engine, short tail, two-element rear wing. |
| Portland | 7/31/88 | 22 | Bobby Rahal | 9 | 1:00.327 (0:57.970) | 20NR | 45 of 97 | |
| Columbus | 10/2/88 | 22 | Bobby Rahal | 3 | 1:31.826 (1:30.500) | 33NR | 13 of 81 | |
| Del Mar | 10/23/88 | 22 | Bobby Rahal | 11 | 1:12.139 (1:06.529) | 5 | 86 of 88 | Last Hendrick Motorsports Corvette GTP to turn IMSA race laps. |

**CHASSIS: HU-8612/03**    **Delivered: July 17, 1987**    **Entrant: Hendrick Motorsports**
**Engine: 3.0-liter (183 CID) Turbo-V6**

| Event | Date | Car Number | Driver(s) | Qualifying Position | Qualifying Time (Pole) | Finish | Laps Completed | Race Comments |
|---|---|---|---|---|---|---|---|---|
| Columbus | 10/4/87 | 52 | Sarel Van Der Merwe<br>Doc Bundy | 4 | 1:32.014<br>(1:29.516) | 22NR | 36 of 81 | First IMSA GTP active suspension car. |

**CHASSIS: HU-8710/01**    **Delivered: October 28, 1987**    **Entrant: Hendrick Motorsports**
**Engine: 6.0-liter (366 CID) V8**

| Event | Date | Car Number | Driver(s) | Qualifying Position | Qualifying Time (Pole) | Finish | Laps Completed | Race Comments |
|---|---|---|---|---|---|---|---|---|
| Miami | 2/28/88 | 52 | Sarel Van Der Merwe<br>Bobby Rahal | 12 | 1:15.960<br>(1:09.802) | 29NR | 54 of 124 | |
| West Palm Beach | 4/21/88 | 52 | Elliott Forbes-Robinson<br>Bobby Rahal | 6 | —<br>(0:58.762) | 13NR | 133 of 149 | |
| Watkins Glen | 7/3/88 | 52 | Sarel Van Der Merwe<br>Elliott Forbes-Robinson | 10 | 1:39.010<br>(1:34.737) | 3 | 90 of 92 | Fitted with short tail and two-element rear wing. |
| Road America | 7/17/88 | 52 | Sarel Van Der Merwe<br>Elliott Forbes-Robinson | 3 | 2:30.506<br>(2:19.487) | 10NR | 72 of 78 | |
| Portland | 7/31/88 | 52 | Sarel Van Der Merwe | 7 | 0:59.965<br>(0:57.970) | 27NR | 7 of 97 | |
| Sears Point | 8/14/88 | 52 | Sarel Van Der Merwe<br>Elliott Forbes-Robinson | 8 | 1:25.595<br>(1:23.139) | 9 | 73 of 75 | |
| San Antonio | 9/4/88 | 52 | Sarel Van Der Merwe<br>Elliott Forbes-Robinson | 4 | 1:05.960<br>(1:04.944) | 17NR | 74 of 142 | |
| Columbus | 10/2/88 | 52 | Sarel Van Der Merwe<br>Elliott Forbes-Robinson | 8 | 1:32.765<br>(1:30.500) | 5 | 80 of 81 | |
| Del Mar | 10/23/88 | 52 | Sarel Van Der Merwe | 3 | 1:07.692<br>(1:06.529) | 24NR | 31 of 88 | |

**CHASSIS: HU-8810/01    Delivered: May 9, 1988    Entrant: Peerless Automotive**
**Engine: 6.0-liter (366 CID) V8**

| Event | Date | Car Number | Driver(s) | Qualifying Position | Qualifying Time (Pole) | Finish | Laps Completed | Race Comments |
|---|---|---|---|---|---|---|---|---|
| Columbus | 10/2/88 | 76 | Jack Baldwin David Hobbs | 7 | 1:32.764 (1:30.500) | 4 | 81 of 81 | |
| Del Mar | 10/23/88 | 76 | Jack Baldwin David Hobbs | 8 | 1:11.568 (1:06.529) | 17NR | 70 of 88 | |
| Tampa | 11/27/88 | 76 | Jack Baldwin David Hobbs | 10 | — (1:07.666) | 10NR | 85 of 117 | Crashed with Ford Probe. |
| West Palm Beach | 4/23/89 | 76 | Jacques Villeneuve Scott Goodyear | 9 | — (0:57.790) | 17NR | 44 of 162 | |
| Mid-Ohio | 6/4/89 | 76 | Jacques Villeneuve Scott Goodyear | 10 | — (1:18.926) | 20NR | 27 of 92 | |
| Watkins Glen | 7/2/89 | 76 | Jacques Villeneuve Scott Goodyear | 10 | — (1:35.878) | 11NR | 81 of 92 | Last Corvette GTP to turn IMSA race laps. |

# Lola Sports Prototypes

**Compiled by John R. Szymanski, Carl Haas Automobile Imports**

| Chassis Number | Delivered to: |
| --- | --- |
| **T-600** | |
| HU-600/01 | Cooke-Woods |
| HU-600/02 | Cooke-Woods |
| HU-600/03 | Tokyo R&D |
| | *(Japan)* |
| HU-600/04 | John Paul |
| HU-600/05 | Chris Cord |
| HU-600/06 | Interscope |
| HU-600/07 | Interscope |
| HU-600/08 | Jamie Mazzota |
| HU-600/09 | Interscope |
| HU-600/10 | GM |
| | *(Corvette GTP prototype)* |
| HU-600/11 | Phil Conte |
| HU-600/12 | Karl Heinz Becker |
| | *(Germany)* |
| **T-610** | |
| HU-610/01 | Lola Racing/Hook |
| | *(Australia)* |
| HU-610/02 | Ralph Cooke |
| **T-616** | |
| HU-616/01 | BFGoodrich |
| HU-616/02 | BFGoodrich |
| HU-616/03 | BFGoodrich |
| HU-616/04 | Polimotor Research/Amoco |

| Chassis Number | Delivered to: |
| --- | --- |
| **T-710** | |
| HU-710/01 | Loaned to GM |
| **T-711** | |
| HU-711/02 | Lee Racing |
| | *(only T-711 built)* |

| Chassis Number | Delivered to: |
| --- | --- |
| **T-810** | |
| HU-810/01 | Electramotive |
| HU-810/02 | Electramotive |
| HU-810/03 | Le Mans Company |
| | *(Japan)* |
| HU-810/04 | Le Mans Company |
| | *(Japan)* |
| **T-8610** | |
| HU-8610/01 | Hendrick Motorsports |
| HU-8610/02 | Hendrick Motorsports |
| HU-8612/03 | GM |
| | *(SN change due to chassis updates and active suspension)* |
| **T-8710** | |
| HU-8710/01 | Hendrick Motorsports |
| **T-8810** | |
| HU-8810/01 | Peerless Racing |
| **T-385** | |
| HU-385/01 | Robin Hamilton |
| HU-385/02 | Robin Hamilton |

## Credits

*Page 33 B, John Pierce photo.*
*Page 38 A, Ford photo.*
*Page 38 B, Ford photo.*
*Page 50 D, Gordon Barrett photo.*
*Page 50 E, Gordon Barrett photo.*
*Page 50 F, Gordon Barrett photo.*
*Page 52 B, Gordon Barrett photo.*
*Page 52 C, John Pierce photo.*
*Page 52 D, Gordon Barrett photo.*
*Page 56 A, John Pierce photo.*
*Page 56 B, John Pierce photo.*
*Page 56 C, John Pierce photo.*
*Page 59, John Pierce photo.*
*Page 59, Chevrolet photo.*
*Page 60 A, John Pierce photo.*
*Page 60 B, John Pierce photo.*
*Page 62, John Pierce photo.*
*Page 68 D, John Pierce photo.*
*Page 70, John Pierce photo.*
*Page 81, John Pierce photo.*
*Page 84 A, Gordon Barrett photo.*
*Page 84 B, Gordon Barrett photo.*
*Page 84 C, Gordon Barrett photo.*
*Page 86 A, Gordon Barrett photo.*
*Page 86 B, Gordon Barrett photo.*
*Page 86 C, Gordon Barrett photo.*
*Page 88 A, Gordon Barrett photo.*
*Page 88 B, Gordon Barrett photo.*
*Page 88 C, Gordon Barrett photo.*
*Page 90 A, Gordon Barrett photo.*
*Page 90 B, Gordon Barrett photo.*
*Page 92, Gordon Barrett photo.*
*Page 98, John Pierce photo.*
*Page 100, John Pierce photo.*
*Page 101 C, Gordon Barrett photo.*
*Page 103, Gordon Barrett photo.*
*Page 104 A, Gordon Barrett photo.*
*Page 104 C, Gordon Barrett photo.*
*Page 106, Gordon Barrett photo.*
*Page 108, Judy Stropus photo.*
*Page 112, Gordon Barrett photo.*
*Page 118, Judy Stropus photo.*
*Page 120 A, Gordon Barrett photo.*
*Page 124 A, Gordon Barrett photo.*
*Page 138, Judy Stropus photo.*
*Page 140, Bob Carson photo.*
*Page 141, Bob Carson photo.*
*Page 142 A, Bob Carson photo.*
*Page 142 B, Bob Carson photo.*
*Page 142 C, Bob Carson photo.*
*Page 144, Judy Stropus photo.*
*Page 146, Judy Stropus photo.*
*Page 148 A, Bob Carson photo.*
*Page 148 B, Bob Carson photo.*
*Page 148 C, Bob Carson photo.*
*All other photos by Alex Gabbard.*